# Be Somebody

# Be Somebody

## A Guide to Achieving Personal Success

Lin Appling

LLA PUBLISHING ✤ JEFFERSON CITY, MISSOURI

*I dedicate this book to my daughter, Linda; my mother, Hettie; my father, Mose; my family; and my belief. I may not know the future and may be confused about the days ahead; however, I cannot be confused about my past. I am certain that God encouraged the present, so I do not need to know the future. I only need to know and believe in God.*

Copyright © 2005 by
LLA Publishing
Jefferson City, Missouri
Printed and bound in the United States of America
All rights reserved
5  4  3  2   09  08  07  06

Library of Congress Control Number: 2005900913

ISBN 978-0-9765249-0-8 (paperback edition)
ISBN 978-0-9765249-1-5 (cloth edition)

∞ This paper meets the requirements of the
American National Standard for Permanence of Paper
for Printed Library Materials, Z39.48, 1984.

Designer: Susan Ferber
Cover photo: Kim Wade, SilverBox Photographers
Printer and binder: Maple-Vail
Typefaces: ITC Giovanni and Formata

# Contents

# Acknowledgments

Thanks to my daughter, Linda, who loves me and supports my dreams. Linda, you are the best!

Thank you, Julie Schroeder, Susan Ferber, Kim Wade, and Jeannie and Mark Worthen. I am honored that you believed in my project and encouraged me through the difficult times. Without your support, this book would have not been possible.

Thanks to my wonderful friends and mentors who believed in me long before they knew that this project was a dream of mine: the Honorable Senator Jean Carnahan and her late husband, the Honorable Governor Mel Carnahan, and Mr. Dick Hanson.

Special thanks to the Honorable Congressman Ike Skelton, Bill Quigg, Jeannie Korman-Meyers, Nancy Gratz, and Bob Robuck and the Central Bank family.

I give thanks to God for stirring my nest and giving me the incredible energy to keep this project alive, and for granting me the privilege of doing the work of encouraging others.

# Introduction

The idea for this book was born out of something my parents said to me when I left home to enter the army. Looking me dead in the eyes, my father told me, "We have great expectations of you." My mother quickly added, "I don't know what to tell you to be. Your father and I have given you our best. I just want you to *be somebody*."

To my mother, "being somebody" was doing what you love; when I was growing up, she would often say, "Lin, remember, you are a child of the King—that in itself makes you somebody. So many of us *say* that we are God's children, but we do not *believe* it." Life should not be a struggle—but if it is, it is because we make it that way.

This book is the story of how I achieved that goal, and it will provide you with a blueprint for how you, too, can achieve your goals—how you can be somebody. It is for anyone who is trying to determine what to do with his or her life. It is for people who know, deep down, that they are not doing all they can do or giving all they can give—to themselves, their families, their careers, or their communities. It is for people who want to make a positive change in their own lives and in the lives of those around them.

I want to help you identify the things you want to do and give you the courage to go out there and do them. We all deserve to do the things we have a passion for. I truly believe that you can achieve your dreams, whether you dream of a new career, fame in the entertainment industry, public office, or a rewarding relationship.

*Be Somebody* gets to the heart of why so many of us fail to achieve the things we want. It identifies the root causes of our failure. Fear, procrastination, indecisiveness, and a lack of patience and confidence can paralyze you. These feelings and beliefs lie inside all of us—but if

1

you don't pursue your dreams, how will you ever know whether you could have succeeded and achieved that which you desire?

Most of us know who we are, where we came from, and where we want to go. That is, we *think* we know it, until someone asks us directly:

—Who are you?
—What do you want?
—Where did you come from?
—Where are you going?
—Who will you be when you arrive?

*Be Somebody* asks these questions and more. It will challenge your beliefs, your habits, and your self-perception. If you follow along step by step, it will change your life for the better, and you can truly "be somebody."

In this world, if you hope to be somebody or do something worthwhile, there will come a time when you must risk it all—everything—with a leap in the dark. You must somehow test your passion for what you want. When you make up your mind to move forward, cut the ropes so that you can sail out into deeper water. As you discover new horizons, opportunities will appear and doors will open that you would have never expected.

When opportunity appears—*take it*. Cross the boundary into a new territory. Step out in faith and don't be afraid. Remember that only a few of us will ever muster up the courage to take the chance to do something extraordinary with our lives. Be careful not to let fear lead you to the dark side of your mind and soul. "That will lead you to anger, hate, and finally suffering."

Remember: *The windows of life, when open, stay open only for a short period of time.* Martin Luther King Jr. wisely told all of us, "the time is always right to do what is right." So do something right for yourself or for someone else. And invest your total faith in the character of our God. Put your trust in him. He will do what he says. Trust him; he makes no mistakes.

Whatever you choose to do in life, commit to it; refuse to run scared, then stick to the task and *become somebody*.

# 1 | Finding Your Way

*Put vim, force, vitality into every movement of your body. Let your very atmosphere be that of [one] who is . . . determined to stand for something, and to be somebody.*

—Orison Swett Marden

## What Do You Want?

Do you realize that most people spend more time planning a Super Bowl party, or a trip to Disney World, than planning for the rest of their lives? How can this be?

—Is it because it is hard?
—Is it because planning your career is no fun?
—Is it because you are afraid you don't have the "right stuff" to succeed?
—Is it because you think you have lots of time?
—Is it because you think it's not important right now?
—Is it because you don't really know what you want or how to go about getting started?

If any of this sounds familiar, then *this book is for you.*

## Finding Your Way

Everything you do and everything you hope to do starts with the picture you paint of yourself. In other words, you are what you think you are. Whatever it is that you love doing is what you have been put here to do. If you are not careful, you can easily be talked out of what

3

deep down, you know you should be doing. If you follow your own beliefs, interests, and passions, you will know what is right for you. This is not easy because most of our parents, teachers, and friends have told us at some point what they think is best for us. But we must hold on to the picture we hold of ourselves, with the self-assurance that what we love to do is what is right for each one of us.

*Ask yourself:* Does this goal fit within my value system? My mother raised me with a strong set of values and a good and healthy self-image, and she always pressed me (in a positive way) to know what I want. She knew that self-knowledge and focus were the keys to success. Please stay the course and don't believe the naysayers. Just keep working on your skills. Believe in yourself, and one day you will see your name among the successful.

At times when I seemed to lack a clear vision in some situation, my father would often ask me, "Boy, do you know what you want?" Without me knowing it, he was building my self-confidence, my self-image, and how I saw myself. My father told me, "Son, when you don't know where you're going, any road will take you there." I didn't appreciate how profound that was until years later, when I realized what he meant: If you don't have a goal, you aren't going anywhere in particular. On the other hand, if you know what you want, that is the first step toward attaining your goal.

When I was young, I didn't know what I wanted or how I was going to get it. I knew what everyone expected of me, but I wasn't sure what I expected of myself. I had no idea what road my life was going to take, and I was really curious about where I was going.

In the seventh grade, I visited Fort Benning, Georgia. I looked around that army post and saw guys in olive green uniforms and shiny boots jumping from a tall paratrooper tower without a net to catch them. These men had courage and discipline and led exciting lives. Suddenly, I knew what it was that I wanted. It was right there in front of me, and I knew it was right for me.

Sometimes it's just that easy. Sometimes your dream is right around the corner, just waiting to be found. All you have to do is open your eyes and accept what is given to you.

I can hear you saying, "Come on Lin, I'm sorry to disagree with you, but deciding what you want to do with your life is just not that easy." You know what? You're right! I have to agree with you. It usually is not that easy.

But I must say that it is not impossible to find your calling. Try not to make it harder than it really is. If you don't try to discover your path, then how will you know what it is? I believe God has a plan for each of us, so prayer or meditation might help you discover your path. And there are a host of people who can help you. For guidance, just look around you at the number of successful individuals in your own community, including your pastor, your banker, your police chief, your teachers, your doctor, and anyone doing work you think you might like to do. Don't be afraid to ask for their help.

You can start by listing all the things that you like to do. Then, make a plan of where you want to be in the future—one year, three years, and five years from now. Also, look back at your past and ask yourself, "How did I get where I am today? What have I done to control my future, and what have I *not* done? Have I just taken life day by day and not given any thought to where I want to be?"

What is it that you love to do? That may be the first clue to finding out what you really want out of life.

If you're not happy with what you are doing now, you have two choices: Learn to love it, or change what you're doing. Your destiny lies in your own hands, not in anyone else's, and if you go through life being miserable with what you're doing, you only have one person to blame: yourself.

Some people go through life unhappy, cranky, and whining, getting up every morning, going to jobs they hate, and working with people with whom they have nothing in common. Why? Because someone expects it of them. You probably know someone like that (it may even be you). You can't make a successful and rewarding career out of doing everything that people expect of you, especially if their expectations don't include your dreams, your goals, or your purpose for being here.

I was lucky to have my parents both show and tell me how important it is to like your work. My father loved farming, so that's what he did, and he was a great success; my mother told me, "Choose to do what makes you happy."

In my present job, I give a monthly orientation seminar for new employees where I ask the questions: "What do you want? Why did you leave your last job? What is your five-year plan? Where do you want or need to be, five years from now?" The answers are almost always the same: "I don't know," or "I'm not sure."

Let me repeat: If you don't know where you're going, you're leaving your future up to chance. What do you want your life to be like? What is your calling, your purpose in life? Can you define it? Can you write it down? Can you articulate it? If not, why not? Let's face it, without answers to these questions you are just dreaming, skipping along, going nowhere. However, with just a little help you can get to where you want to be. I would like to encourage you to focus on your expectations, your attitude, your beliefs, and your self-confidence. Without well-defined goals, your life is just a toss-up—a flip of the coin.

## My Family's Advice

When you set out to be somebody, to make or remake yourself into a new image, you have to take into account your roots. Of course I don't know your roots, and I don't know where you come from or where you want to go. I know we all come from different circumstances. However, let's stop right here. I would like to speak directly to those of you who came from poor neighborhoods, from broken families, or had abusive parents. This kind of background has played a major role in who you are today.

At this point I don't want to be misunderstood. We all have to focus on what we want—this process challenges all of us. I have spent the last fifteen years studying successful people, and my experience has shown me that the middle class and the privileged are also challenged by the need to focus on what they want to do with their lives. We all need to learn how to control our mental focus.

But if you come from particularly challenging circumstances, I want you to pay special attention at this point: I come from a family of fourteen; I grew up in a rural community in Georgia, and my parents were farmers. I have experienced similar stumbling blocks. One of the major reasons that I wrote this book was to encourage you to face your fears and your difficulties and to embrace change. Forget about where you've been and what your present situation is; focus on where you want to go.

Remember, there is no single "right way" to achieve success—each of us is a different person who is starting from a different point in life and is headed for different destinations. Don't be afraid of your fears; don't run scared. If you have not tried, you have not lived. Stay flexible and open. Who knows when lightning may strike? *Remember that faith can move mountains.*

Family is important to me and I worried that my family wouldn't understand my choice in life. After all, the army was *not* their goal for me. I think that my father expected that I would remain in Georgia because few people we knew had ever served in the military. My father wanted me to finish college with a major in agriculture and seek employment with the federal government in the field of conservation. My parents never imagined I would become an officer in the U.S. Army. But I knew the roads they had in mind weren't the ones I wanted to take. Needless to say, my parents were surprised when I announced that I was going to enlist in the army.

My father took my decision in stride, however, and sat down to tell me a few things, which I consider some of the greatest advice I've ever gotten. He told me:

—"Hang around with winners";
—"Buy yourself a Big Ben alarm clock"; and
—"Take out your own trash and wash your own dishes, because no one else will do it for you."

*What did he mean when he said these things?* Just this:

**Hang around with winners.** Who you hang around with helps determine who you are. If you hang around with people with good habits—such as getting up early, working hard, treating people fairly, and not smoking—you will acquire those habits if you want them, and it will be easier to acquire them because the people around you are doing the same thing. We are, after all, creatures of habit.

We all model after one another. The company you keep will become a part of your life and your lifestyle. Surround yourself with people who will improve, encourage, or help you in some way; people who have only positive things to say and who live positive lives. Hang around with those who have already achieved the thing that is *your* dream or *your* goal, and chances are, you will achieve it, too.

**Buy yourself a Big Ben alarm clock.** An alarm clock wakes you up. You rely on it, and yourself, to get where you're going when you need to be there. Just as it's important to be on time for work and for appointments with others, it's important to make a schedule for your life and to meet your own deadlines. Write down your goals for where you want to be, and what you want to be doing, one year, two to three years, and three to five years from now. You will revisit this plan many times, and more than likely you will change it often. But without a blueprint of where you want to go, you'll never get there.

Once you have written down your goals in the important areas of your life (such as spiritual, professional, and family), the hard work has just begun, because you still have to map out your strategy for accomplishing your goals. You must still make a plan.

**Take out your own trash and wash your own dishes.** When you make a mess, clean it up. And I'm not talking about just housework. I'm talking about *everything* you do. If you mess something up, make it right. That's called taking responsibility, and you have to do that to succeed.

Doing what you love is fine, but don't make anyone else clean up after you. There was someone at an office I worked in who always seemed to jam up the photocopier so badly it was unusable, and then he would just walk away from it, leaving it like that so that someone else had to fix the problem before anyone else could use the machine. Don't do that. Don't make others responsible for you. Learn to do your own job without relying on others to do something for you. If you're stuck and need help, fine, but do whatever it takes not to have to do that very often.

Truly successful people make mistakes just like everyone else, but they fix whatever went wrong before moving on. That's something you can learn. If something goes really wrong in your life, fix it, even if it means facing a harsh consequence like losing your job or going to court. Consequences can be hard, but leaving things undone in your life keeps the problem hanging over your head.

# Making It Happen

When I left home, I knew that the one thing I could not do was return as a failure, no matter where my life led me. I would be somebody and make my parents proud. My decision to do this was a driving force in my life. I will always be thankful to my mother and father for giving me that goal. It was the thing that kept me going many times when I wanted to give up.

Sometimes it was hard, and sometimes I got more (or less) than I bargained for from the choices I made—but I made those choices, I took what came as a result, and I always strived for what I wanted.

Can you "make it happen"? Can you learn to do what you love, and love what you do? What do you think? In my more than forty years of managing people, I've heard over and over again, "Lin, I'm not smart enough" (or "strong enough," or "talented enough") "to live my dreams." "I don't have what it takes." "I've never had a chance." "I am the wrong color" (or "sex," or "age"). "I was raised on the wrong side of town."

In response, I ask, "What makes me different? *I* represent everything you have said. You have everything you need to get what you want. The difference between success and failure is determination."

*You* are the only one who has what it takes to make your dreams come true. Once you decide to do it, it's up to you to make it happen. Of course, making the decision to do something extraordinary with your life is not enough by itself to get you through the difficult years, but it is the most *important* part.

The first time I ever jumped out of an aircraft, it was easy. Does that surprise you? *It was easy.* The jumpmaster pointed at me, I stood up, and I went out the door at fourteen thousand feet.

Of course, I'd made the same kind of jump hundreds of times previously, on the ground, and thousands of times in my imagination. I'd jumped out of that airplane so many times in my mind—each time imagining that I was high up in the air, looking down on a wide landscape thousands of feet below—so that when the time came,

I went out just like that. I went without fear, taking a leap of faith, because I *knew* I could do it. Without that faith, I might have failed.

If I have it in me to step out that door with nothing more than faith that I will be safe, I can tell you that *you* have it in you to do whatever you need to do to make your dream come true, to achieve your goal, and to become the person you want to be.

You do not have to graduate from Harvard or MIT or Cal Tech to make it to the top. You don't have to be the richest, the smartest, the funniest, the most talented, or even the most popular person on the planet. You don't have to be the "most" anything. You just have to know what you want, and you have to want it badly enough to work for it and never give up on making it become a reality.

Where I come from—in rural Georgia and in a thirty-year career in the army—it was not necessarily the smartest guy who won, but the persistent and humble guy who believed in himself. I can tell you're thinking, "Okay, Lin. I can understand persistence. 'Don't give up,' 'never stop trying,' and all that. But the most *humble?* I don't get it."

*Humble* also means *teachable*, because if you're a humble person, you know you still have things to learn. You know that other people can be right and that you can be wrong. If you can pay attention to what life has to teach you, you will go a long way.

I paid attention to what my parents said to me when I left home to join the U.S. army: "Do what you love, and love what you do." And I lived my life by them. Now, I'm living my dream.

*You can live yours, too.*

## Exercise:

Setting and achieving your goals is like planting a field—you will only harvest what you plant and cultivate. So, before you go any further in this book, let's start to find out what it is you really and truly want to do with your life. Make a list of everything. Include anything that you've ever wanted to do. Think about your life goals and what you're good at. Think about what your purpose for being here is.

_____

_____

_____

_____

_____

_____

_____

_____

_____

_____

_____

_____

_____

Next, write down your goals for where you want to be, and what you want to be doing one year, three years, and five years from now. These goals can relate to your family, your profession, or your finances, or they could be something of personal importance to you.

**One-year goals:** _____

_____

**Three-year goals:** _____

_____

_____

_____

_____

_____

_____

_____

_____

_____

_____

_____

_____

_____

_____

**Five-year goals:** _____

_____

_____

_____

_____

_____

_____

_____

_____

_____

_____

_____

_____

_____

# 2 | Fueling the Fire Within

*I always wanted to be somebody, but I should have been more specific.*

—Lily Tomlin

## Digging Up Your Dream

Human beings have come a long way over the last few centuries. We've developed technologies, improved medicines, traveled to the moon. We've gained awesome power over the earth, especially considering our humble beginnings. Our society has developed to the point where no one person can contain the knowledge of everything we've learned, discovered, or invented. Yet each of us has certain knowledge and some special talent that allows us to contribute to the whole of society. Each of us has the power within ourselves to become someone or to do something extraordinary with our lives.

Unfortunately, there are three things at which we've all become absolutely brilliant: lying to ourselves, beating ourselves up, and burying our dreams.

Each of these things keeps us from becoming the person we want to be, but the one I think is most important, and perhaps our greatest tragedy, is burying our dreams, or becoming conditioned to accept or "make do" with what we have or what we have become. When we acquiesce to our circumstances, swallowing whatever life serves us, we are settling for the crumbs that fall from the table instead of eating the meal we deserve.

That is why it so important to know what it is you want out of life. Remember, making a solid decision about what you want is not as easy as it sounds. Take it from me, it is tough. With so many distractions, it is a hard thing to line up your life with your desires. But the point that I want you to remember is that it is *not impossible.*

Sometimes it becomes very painful to talk about, to hope for what we really want, because we all know that things could happen—we could get distracted, fate might intervene—and we fear we will never get it. *Fear* is one of the major reasons we do not venture to obtain the things we want. When you announce to the world that you want to be a motivational speaker—which is the one thing *I* truly want— when you make this known, you are leaving your flanks open and vulnerable to ridicule—especially if you do not succeed. Anytime you drive down your stake and say, "I am going to do this; it is my goal and passion; it is my purpose," you are exposed. If you fail or are rejected, it cuts right down to the bone, and it hurts. So what we do is try to play it safe by straddling the fence, by trying to play both ends against the middle.

Take it from me, I've tried that, and it does not work. You have to cut the ropes and move away from the dock. Life has taught me over and over again that fear has a much greater grip on your dreams immediately after you make the commitment than ever before. Be prepared for this. It feels risky, being true to yourself. You have to have courage that your desires will lead you toward your goal.

One of the major points that I have taken from Viktor E. Frankl's book *Man's Search for Meaning* comes from his experience in surviving the death camps in Germany during World War II. His faith kept him going; he believed that everyone has a unique calling in life, no matter what the circumstances. Everyone has some gift to make the world a better place. When a man stops believing, he will stop caring. Hope is sometimes the only thing we have to hold onto. I think Frankl's memoir should be required reading for all of us.

Getting in touch with what you really, really want is not easy. I wish I could tell you there is a simple set of rules, steps, and principles that everyone can follow to achieve guaranteed success, but there is no such thing. While there are basic guidelines to play by, and things you can do to make true success come more easily, it will be different for each of us.

The fundamental idea, however, is to find what you love to do—

discover what gives life meaning for you—and then have the intestinal fortitude and the stamina to go after it.

It makes no difference how you find out what you love to do. But whatever it is, it's a thing that will give you joy, peace, pleasure, love, and happiness, something that will bring you to the end of your life with pride behind you, happiness around you, and love and hope before you.

In this book I give you a road map and guidelines to follow to your individual success and happiness. If you follow the map, be prepared for an occasional detour; if this is the case, stop and ask for directions whenever you feel lost, and yes, be willing to risk failure. Be willing to change your direction along the route, but don't quit or give up. Have faith that you will arrive at your destination.

These principles have worked for me. My good days, my successes, and my will to win have always overpowered any disappointments and failures, and my occasional impulse to give up.

You must set your compass and stay on course; focus on your goal; envision it. Remember to keep your eyes on the prize, because if you do not plan your life, someone else, or some situation, will. Know what you want to do. Have a plan and work it. Be careful how you live and how you spend your time. Make the most of your life, because your time *is* your life, and your life is controlled by your time. If you are going through this world, why not make the best of it and choose to be happy and successful. *Why not?*

# The Road Map

There are markers on the road map, but you must make them for yourself. Here is how to make them:

—Analyze your life and desires, and determine what you want.
—Have the courage to ask for what you want.
—Get started, stay flexible, and don't quit.

You have to know what you want, and you can't be afraid to ask for it or for help in getting it. Knowing what you want is the first and most important step toward doing what you love and loving what you do. Without a goal of some kind—an idea of where and who you want to be—you may not be able to find the path you want to take. Remember what my father told me? He said, "If you don't know where you're going, any road will take you there." You have to know where you're going. And you don't even necessarily have to know exactly *what* you want to be; you just have to know *who* you want to be. What kind of person will you need to become to make your dreams come true?

So you want to get jump-started, but you still don't truly know what it is that you want out of life. That doesn't mean you're weak or lacking; sometimes we all need a little help to get things rolling. This book will help you get there.

You know what? If the truth were known, most of us don't really know what we want. Join the crowd—you're in the majority. But it doesn't have to be that way. Some of us have always done what was expected of us. Some of us have lived our lives coasting, accepting what was given to us without thinking about the road ahead, grateful for the crumbs that have fallen from the table. Still others have "sacrificed" our own futures, not pursuing the dreams we have in order to "take care of" or "be there" for some other person or group of persons—such as a parent, a child, or a spouse.

And some people are simply clueless about why life is passing them by.

Do you fit into one of these categories? Stop for a minute and ask yourself these questions: How are you ever going to find out what you want from life? Where do you find your purpose, your dream, your goal? Does it seem hopeless? Hold on! Don't tune me out. I can help you. If you give me the opportunity, I can help you dig deep inside to ignite that fire within you.

*Let's go dream hunting.*

## Identify What You Want

What you need to find is your life purpose or calling, that one thing that most makes you happy. If you can't name it right away, then welcome to the club! You're not alone, believe me. You are standing in the middle of a large crowd of people, all in the same position, waiting for life to hand them something or accepting what's already been handed to them. To be somebody, you have to step away from the crowd and take control of your own destiny. It's time to decide who and what you want to be.

I can hear some of you saying, "Lin, I don't have a dream. There's nothing I want that's different than what I have. I'm doing just fine." Congratulations! That's great, and I'm happy to hear it.

But if you're like the rest of us, you have a dream of something different, something better. Most people do, even those who may look like they have it all—yes, even those people who say they are happy right where they are! If you didn't believe there was more out there to see and do, you wouldn't be reading this book. There is something you want more than anything else, even if you don't know or won't admit to yourself what it is. Think about it. What is it that wakes you up at night with that gut-wrenching ache, when you know that other people are doing it instead of you? What is it that brings tears to your eyes when you see someone else doing it, and you know deep in your heart that you could do it too—maybe better? What is it that truly makes you happy?

You know what I'm talking about. It's that one thing that you always wished you could be doing as a job or career, because you'd be having so much fun at it you'd never *really* have to work again— instead, people would be paying you to do what you love. Those who are truly doing what they love are being paid, so it doesn't even feel like work. Why spend your life toiling in unhappiness? Don't let yourself arrive at retirement where you say to yourself, "I should've" or "I could've."

What is the one thing that wakes you up at night when you dream of it? What is it that eats at your soul because you're not doing it? What is the one thing that would make you happy? What is it?

Usually, it's that thing where you say, "Yeah, but that was a stupid kid's dream."

If you want it, it's not stupid. If you want to learn how to get it, read on.

And if you still don't know what it is, read on.

Who are you? Who are you deep down inside? Do you really know? This is a hard question, because some of us really don't know. Some of us aren't in touch with ourselves; we don't know anymore what makes us happy, or we live life just to "make it through another day."

I think "making it through another day" is one of the biggest tragedies in the world, because those of us who say that—and I have been one of those people myself—are wishing our lives *away.* When we tell ourselves, "If I can just make it through today," or "till Friday," or "till next September," we are spending our precious time without gaining anything back. Our lives are gifts we receive when we are born; our time off from work is time we buy through our daily labor. Time is like a dollar bill: You earned it, worked hard for it, and can spend it any way you want—but you can only spend it once. You have to invest your time wisely. Make sure you get a return on your investment, or it will all go away for nothing. At that point, you've made the sour old saying "Life's hard, and then you die" come true.

It doesn't have to be that way, though, because the reverse can also be true: "Life's wonderful, because I made it wonderful. I'm working on my dream, and success is on its way."

But to make that happen, first you have to find out who you really are and what your dream is.

# Find Out Who You Are

Have you ever noticed that people who are happy will almost always tell you about their profession when you meet them? After they tell you their names, they'll say, "I own a pet store"; "I'm a paramedic with the hospital"; or "I'm a freelance photographer."

It's a fact that we all have something we're good at, something that makes us happy, something we have a passion for. We are all born with a talent for something, and it's almost always true that we enjoy doing the things we have a talent for. I'm not saying that you're born with the ability to play the piano or paint a masterpiece the minute you set your hand to it. What I'm telling you is that you *can* do those things, if you want to and you like doing it, if you take your natural talent and make it work for you. No matter what your goal, remember: "Easy" is *not* an option. Truly, you were born with a gift. You have it. You just have to *develop* it.

Some people don't know what their dream is because they don't

# Missouri's Ike

Ike Skelton knew at the age of fourteen that he would be a congressman. The year was 1946, and Ike was helping his father campaign for a seat in Congress. After a long struggle, Ike's father came in second in a three-way primary. At that time, Ike knew in his subconscious, in his heart of hearts, that he'd follow in his father's footsteps and run for office one day himself. He'd been around politics all his life, and it just seemed the natural thing to do.

But first, he prepared himself with the usual prerequisites for achieving his goal: he had to go to college, graduate from law school, and obtain a position practicing law. Ike did all three. And he not only graduated in record time, but also became the prosecuting attorney of his home county at the age of twenty-four, right out of law school. A remarkable achievement in itself.

But Ike wasn't about to stop there.

After serving two terms as prosecutor and practicing law with his father for several years, he ran for public office: "I was a racehorse looking for a race, and I ran in the state senate. I won that by 348 votes against the incumbent."

In 1959, at the age of twenty-eight, he nearly ran for U.S. Congress when an incumbent died leaving an open position, but due to party splits that year, he did not win the nomination.

Interestingly, Skelton is not upset at that loss; he is grateful: "It was a good thing [that] . . . I did not get it, because I would not have gotten to practice law with my father, which was a real highlight."

In 1976, he ran again for Congress, one of nine contenders in the primary, including two other state senators. He won his primary, doing well throughout his district, which included Kansas City, and he carried all but one rural county. In the general election, he ran against the mayor of Independence and won.

Ike's dedication to his work has earned him the esteem of his district's constituents and of his colleagues in Congress. He has represented Missouri's Fourth Congressional District in the U.S. House of Representatives since 1977. It's not an easy job, but it gives him great satisfaction: "This is a tough business, but I like what I do. If you like what you do, it's not work."

Ike describes his deep-rooted faith, too. He has no other explanation for it. He attributes much of his success to faith and good friends. "I have been . . . fortunate to have great friends when I need to talk to somebody."

He wants to encourage everyone he meets. Everyone has experienced hardship in some form, and he, too, has had his share of adversity. He wants to share his success story with "young and old" to show them that if he can achieve his dreams, they can too. It can happen.

It happened to him. He knew it would, and it did.

know who they are. If you make important life decisions without knowing who you are, you may wake up one day deeply unfulfilled, realizing you're wasting your life and possibly hurting others in the process. I have a close friend who married her sweetheart and thought she was very happy until she woke up one day and realized she had no idea who she really was. It had gotten to the point where she felt she had to get a divorce. It was a huge blow to her family, but that's not really my point. The point is, she had subsumed her entire personality into her husband and his life. She'd given up everything she was in order to be with him, and in the end, she realized the mistake she had made.

Living someone else's dream is never a good thing.

I know many people who are trying to be something they're not, just to make someone else happy. People do it all the time, for their husband or wife, for their parents, their children, even their boss. Even if this is the case with you, calm down! You don't necessarily need a divorce or anything that drastic in order to find yourself. All you have to do is find out what you like and who you really are.

So ask yourself: "Am I happy? Do I really enjoy doing this?"

Once you know what you really want to do, you can start to work on making it happen.

So let's try this: *Write down ten activities you engage in weekly.* I don't mean the things you have to do, like washing dishes or picking up the kids. I mean stuff you do on a regular basis, when you have a choice of things to do—things like going to the mall, cross-stitching, or working in the garage. Don't read on without doing this!

☐ _____

☐ _____

☐ _____

☐ _____

☐ _____

☐ _____

☐ _____

☐ _____

☐ _____

☐ _____

Okay. Now, go back and mark an X next to those activities you really enjoy. We're being honest, remember?

If there's nothing you really enjoy, you've got some soul-searching to do.

I want you to carefully consider why you're in the situation you're in. If you come up with the words "I don't know," you have some dream hunting to do. Go back to your list of things you like (or would like) to do, or that others have said you're good at, at the end of Chapter 1. Which of those things do you have a passion for? Which have you never tried?

If you still don't know, then it's time to try new things and find out what you enjoy. Check out a new craft or sport, visit the library for unusual ideas, and if you find yourself saying, "Hey, that looks like fun," your assignment is to try that.

It won't be too long before you learn what it is you want to do with your life.

And don't you *dare* say, "It's too late for that" or "I could never do that." Starting right now, language like this is no longer for you. It may not be easy, and there may be obstacles, but you can make your dream work for you, no matter who you are, if you believe that you can do it.

So no negative thinking.

Once you've begun to try new things, you'll start finding out what you're good at and enjoy. I firmly believe that once you've found out what you're good at, you'll quickly find out if that's what you love and if it is your "burning passion." It could be something as wild as skydiving or snowboarding, or something less "gonzo" and more serene, like drawing, writing, computer programming, or accounting.

And if you are still saying, "I'm too dumb" or "too old" for that, or "I'd enjoy that, but it's not for me," skip directly—*right now!*—to Chapter 4. We need to talk.

If you find out what you're good at, you'll learn who you are inside. You'll learn what makes you happy. Once you learn what makes you happy, you have a goal—you know what your purpose in life should be.

# Talk to Yourself

For those of you who are still clueless about your dream, the main question in this chapter is: Are you happy? Honesty is important here. Look into the mirror—really, right now—get up, find a mirror, and look at yourself: look directly into your eyes, and ask yourself: "Am I happy with who I am? Am I satisfied with what I'm doing?" Since you've got no one to impress, no one to lie to, no one who needs to think you're something different than you are, you can tell the truth. Ask yourself: "Am I happy?" If you answer in the negative, then the next question is: "Why not?"

—Are you happy getting up in the morning and living the life you lead?

—Are you happy going to work and doing the job you do with the people you work with?

—Are you happy with the amount of money you're receiving, driving the car you drive, living in the place you live?

—Are you happy going home to your current living situation?

—Are you happy with yourself going to bed at night? Do you never think about something different, something more rewarding, something more *fun?*

If the answer to any one of these questions is no, something is missing—is it possible that you're not living your dream? Without knowing what it is, you can't work toward achieving it. *You can do better.*

# What Did You Leave Behind?

For those of you who have sacrificed your dreams for something or someone else, you know who you are. And you also know what dream you've given up on. Make no mistake about this: *You know—* your gut tells you every day of your life. Be honest with yourself.

For some of you, the sacrifice took place so long ago, you may not even remember what your dream was. Or you may think it was a "stupid kid's dream."

Read my lips: *No, it wasn't.* There are no stupid kid dreams. It is true that there are some dreams that just can't be fulfilled, but dreams are *never* stupid. I have a friend who always wanted to be an astronaut when he was a kid. He parked himself for hours in front of the TV, watching the astronauts, their training, their space flights, moon landings, explorations, and experiments. He could quote to you all the names of the astronauts, which flights they were on, and in what years. In the days before videos and DVDs, he audiotaped all fifteen hours of the 1975 Apollo-Soyuz linkup. And he listened to it more than once! He watched it all again on PBS in 1994 when they re-broadcast all the footage of the moon shots, and he watched all of HBO's fictional *From the Earth to the Moon* broadcasts in 1998.

Unfortunately, this man is an epileptic and has bad eyes. Because of his physical limitations, the Air Force would not take him, so he could not learn to be a pilot in order to study in space. Was that the end of his dream?

No! He continued studying astronomy and pursued other dreams. He uses what he's learned about astronauts and astronomy to write science fiction. So he's not an astronaut . . . but is he happy? Yes, he is. So you see, there really are no "foolish kid dreams," only dreams that you may not be able to pursue at the moment. And there is always a way to keep at least a part of them with you.

*Never give up your dreams.* You never know when something might happen to make them come true. When it's least expected, the opportunity will present itself or someone will come into your life to get you jump-started. Hang in there and keep looking and asking. Your dream is buried closer than you think. Dig it up!

Now, those of you who are older and gave up dancing when you were twelve, and those of you who want to be football players are all ready to give me a hundred excuses why you can't ever take it up again. But that's all they are: excuses. There may be limitations, but dreams can still come true, sometimes in unexpected ways—Why not teach dance, or coach a group of children?

I know a woman who sacrificed her dream for her family. She stopped playing the trumpet in order to get married, and even after she got divorced, she didn't take it up again. Why? She said it was "silly." But she still takes out her case and wistfully puts the trumpet together every once in a while, plays a note or two, then cleans it and replaces it in its case. When I ask her why she doesn't play, she says, "I don't 'have it' anymore."

Get out of town: She still has it! She's giving herself excuses, just like we all do. And she'll never have "it" again until she realizes that excuses will never get her anywhere but where she is right now. And if she's not happy, she has only herself to blame. You have to take control of your own life, give up the excuses, and get on with what you love to do. But you need to know what it is you want to do.

So let's do this: *In the space below, list what you've given up.* I don't care what you gave it up for; that's not important here. It is very likely that the circumstances that led you to give up your dream may no longer exist. And if they do, ask yourself this question, "Is it worth it?" At some level, it might actually be worth it, because you've basically made a trade and hopefully you've gotten something in return for putting your dream on hold. But remember the other question, the main question: "Am I happy?" Because if you think about it, if *you* aren't happy, how happy are the people around you?

If there is some dream you gave up, write down what it was and what it meant to you at the time you gave it up.

_____

_____

_____

---

---

---

---

---

---

I'm going to ask you again: Was it worth it? And if it was, is it still worth it? There is the classic story of the father who gives up his dream of being a painter to have a family. If you have to give something up, a family is a good tradeoff. But are you still working on your family, or have they grown and gone and you're still wishing and dreaming?

Are you still giving me excuses? If you're still spouting reasons why you can't live your dream, remember that until you say, "Yes, I want to live my dream," you're not going anywhere. I can't help you until you know what you want to do.

Give yourself permission. Ready? Say it with me: "I can *do* it." One more time, with feeling: *"I can do it!"*

If you believe it, you *can* do it. That's all there is to starting.

First you need to decide what you want. Then, having made that decision, make the commitment to follow your dream. And after that comes the easy part: Get *fired up* about it! That is what this book is about.

We all have dreams. All we have to do is pay attention to what they are and have the courage to ask for what we want. Look for your dream. Define it, find it, play with it—seize it. Make it yours—take it home with you; bring it to bed with you. Start to live, breathe, and feel it; eat, drink, and sleep it; develop your passion for it. And *believe that you can do it.* Then you can truly be on your way to being somebody!

# 3 | Self-Analysis: What Do You Bring to the Table?

*My philosophy is that only you are responsible for your life, but doing the best at this moment puts you in the best place for the next moment.*

—Oprah Winfrey

Now, let's see if we can put into practice some of the things we've learned so far. I'm going to walk you through some questions—some will be hard. I'm going to ask you to do something very difficult: You have to answer these questions with complete honesty. All the suggestions and exercises in here are based on an honest appraisal of who you are and what you want.

Don't worry. I'm not going to make you do all the work here. I'll show you examples of what I mean when I ask you a specific question, and walk you through the questions and some sample answers from my life. But I need you to answer honestly. You don't need to worry about telling me your secrets—I'm not really here, remember? These are my words in a book. The only one here is you. The only one you really have to be honest with is you. It's hard, but you can do it. *Let's begin.*

What you get out of this chapter depends solely on how honestly you answer the questions I'll ask you. And remember, what you get out of the rest of this book depends on what you learn about yourself from this chapter.

You don't even have to write your answers here. Go grab a yellow legal pad and a red felt-tip pen if you don't like writing in the book.

*Are you ready?*

# What Do You Want?

This is the most important question you will have to answer. The answer is critical to everything else you will ever do in life, because it will give you a goal or a destination, and once you have that, you can map your journey. Remember what my father said—if you don't know where you're going, any road will take you there. This is how you know where you're going. We've been talking about this for a while; now it's time to put it into writing.

Several years ago, I started working for the State of Missouri. It was a good job, I was doing fine, the pay was excellent—in fact, it was the highest-paying job I'd ever had. I had a ton of respect from my coworkers, but I was missing something. I knew exactly what it was, and I knew exactly what I wanted. Everything I had ever done was leading me to my dream of being a motivational speaker; it was like taking a series of connecting flights, each one leading me closer to my final destination.

I have always dreamed of using my words to help others be more successful. My idea of a sense of accomplishment is to live my dream by helping others to find and live theirs. I would wake up at night with the inspiring words of other speakers in my mind, and I knew, just knew, that I could do it just as well as they could—maybe better. But for fifteen years, I half-buried my dream, pursuing it on and off, one foot in the door and one out, rooted in a safe place. I would ask myself: If other people can do it—go from being a "nobody" to being *somebody*—why can't I?

After wrestling with it for a while, I decided to take a leap of faith: I went out and began taking all the speaking engagements I could get. And it snowballed from there! Because I decided on what I wanted, I was able to find the strength in myself to go out and do it. Just do it. As my parents said, "do what you love and love what you do"—and success will show up precisely on time.

Before you can tap into that strength in yourself, you have to know where you want to go. The goal itself will give you strength, faith, and courage to step out and make your dreams come true. If you can set that goal and have the self-confidence to achieve it, you will be successful—not just in terms of money or power, but successful because you are finally able to "do what you love and love what you do." And that's a good thing.

Now, before we go on, I want you to articulate what you want by simply finishing a sentence that begins with "I want to be . . . ," or "I want to travel to . . . ," or "I want to accomplish . . ." in the space below, right under mine. It will help if you are as specific as possible, because you'll use this sentence to chart the course ahead. What is it that you want out of life? What is your purpose, your dream, your passion? If you need to, take a little time to think about it, meditate, whatever will help you focus all your desires into one phrase. Then write it down.

**Example:**

Lin: I want to be a dynamic motivational speaker and writer; I want to help other people get from where they are to where they want to be.
You: I want to . . .

_____

_____

_____

# What You Take with You

A current buzzword is "baggage." Everyone has been using it; you've probably heard it on television or the radio, or even from the people sitting in the next booth at McDonald's. This word is useful because we all have some "baggage" to carry around—and it doesn't have anything to do with the luggage you check through at the airport. "Baggage" is the remnants of your past that you lug around, for better or worse, and it has a lot to do with the kind of person you are today.

To achieve your goals, you must have a good, clear picture of who you are right now, as well as where you've been. How much baggage are you carrying around? How much of it do you want to take with you on your journey? It's time to find out. The next few questions are designed to help you decide what you should take with you, and how much you should let go of.

Another thing you will take with you is your character. As you embark on your journey to success, you can use the strengths of your personality as assets.

What is character? Somebody once told me, "character is what you are when you are all alone and in the dark." And my father always told me that "hard times build character." Most of us have experienced and will experience hard times in our lives. They do occur, and when they do, our lives can become very difficult. Life is not always "fair." Sometimes adversity comes to us seemingly by chance, like being in the wrong place at the wrong time, and there's nothing we can do about it but rely on our wits, our family and friends, and the inner strength of our character.

So in addition to showing the nature and extent of your "baggage," the next several questions are designed to reveal your character. I don't know you, so I can't tell you who you are. How you answer these questions will show you who you are and what you've learned. I've given you examples of my answers to show you what kind of answers will help you discover your true self. I'll lead off each set of questions with a story from my own life as an illustration.

## What's the most difficult thing you've had to face?

As a soldier, I had to go to Vietnam, as my mother feared, and face a real enemy whose mission was to kill me. From the moment I stepped off the plane in Southeast Asia, I was aware of the danger. But I also knew I would fight for my country and that the best way to get through the confrontation was to face my fear straight on.

There, I learned the difference between the hero and the coward. The hero takes action while the coward stands still. You have to decide which you will be—will you grab hold of what you want and make it happen, or will you wait for life to happen to you and take whatever comes? You know which way is right if you really want to achieve your goals. Take the risk, burn your bridges behind you, make the commitment, and you are halfway there.

Vietnam and going to Airborne and Officer Candidate School were all difficult choices I made. Each of these endeavors was hard, but each brought me one step closer to being who I wanted to be.

Quitting was never an option for me, because I was determined to be somebody, to make my family proud, and to live the life I'd always wanted. "Easy" was not an option, either.

Below, I want you to describe one of the most difficult events you've ever faced, and what you learned from it. The learning we're talking about could be something about yourself, something about human nature, or something about the condition of mankind on this planet.

For example, my first airplane jump, which I've already talked a little bit about, was difficult for me, but it was also fun, and I learned that I had the courage to do it. It didn't hurt or kill me, and it was something I really wanted to do. Over the jump zone, the green light came on, and I was the first out the door. I jumped, landed, and walked off the field. A perfect jump.

Being in the army was a learning experience, but finding out I could step out of an airplane into the wide open sky proved to me that I had what it takes to do what I wanted to do with my life. That was a lesson worth learning, and I was fortunate to learn it so early in life. Now it's your turn.

Event: _____

Lesson: _____

_____

_____

_____

_____

## What's the saddest thing you've ever faced?

Although it may not seem so at the time, you can also learn from the bad things that happen to you, or when something goes wrong in an unexpected way. When I stood in my front yard watching my wife drive away, I knew that my world had changed irreversibly and that this painful moment would stay with me forever. It seemed like everything I'd ever loved, except my daughter, was in that car. I couldn't believe my wife was leaving. I had tried to change for her, I had worked so hard to become the person she wanted me to be, and it hadn't made any difference in the long run. My life was empty; I had failed. My daughter and I were forced to face the world together.

My heart broke that day, and for a long time I didn't think I was ever going to get over it. Yet years later, I realized that I had healed. It didn't happen immediately, but I recovered. What's more, I learned two very important things from that experience.

First, I learned that you can't change someone else; you can only change yourself. You can improve yourself, and the people around you will probably react to that change, whether for good or bad. But you can't make others happy if you're not happy yourself. And if your best is not good enough for them or not important to them, then you probably don't need to be around them.

Second, I learned that forgiveness takes care of a lot of things in your life. I found that many aspects of my life started to correct themselves once I finally understood that she had the right to leave me. It was her choice. And that's what life is all about: making choices. She had to be the one to decide what she felt was best for her. Many years passed before I could deal with this, but once I did, I was able to finally forgive her. She did what she had to do, and I forgave her for the ill effect it happened to have had on me. I wrote her a letter. I let go of the anger and resentment I'd carried with me all that time.

Once I did, everything in my life improved. The light became brighter. It was like walking out of darkness into daylight.

Sadness has affected me more than once through the people I love. My mother spent more than five years lying in a bed, unable to even roll over. She could only move her head from side to side, and even that was difficult. It hurt me to see her in that condition, but it also made me realize a few things.

First, I learned that no matter who you are, you cannot escape the tough times that will come into your life.

Second, I learned that life really is shorter than you think, and "fairness" is really not an issue. We need to make up our minds to live our lives to the fullest every day. Go out and do what you love. That's really all you have to do; the rest will fall into place if you can do that one thing.

*Now, it's your turn.* What's the saddest thing you've ever been through, and what did you take away from it?

Event: _____

Lesson: _____

_____

_____

_____

_____

_____

## What event in your life produced the most adversity and the biggest reward?

The army was everything I had for a large part of my life. After I got out of the army, I got fired from the very first job I had. It was a hard experience, and I was filled with anxiety about what would happen to me: What would I do to earn a living? This experience also benefited me in some interesting ways.

Most important, I learned—eventually—that being fired was the best thing that ever happened to me. There were three reasons why this was so: I did not like the job; I did not like the people I had to work with; and I wanted more.

As it turned out, four months after my termination, the governor of Missouri appointed me to his staff, which was a major step up for me. At that point, I was able to look back at my former employment without bitterness, because I was able to take something of value away from that experience, knowing that my former bosses had inadvertently done me a favor.

By overcoming this setback, I learned not to sweat the small things in life. Something will always work out if you are willing to work for it. I was willing, and I went above and beyond what that first job would have given me.

Again, it's your turn. Write down something difficult you had to go through that produced a high reward, and what you learned from it.

Event: _____

Lesson: _____

_____

_____

_____

_____

_____

_____

## What event in your life produced the biggest reward—with or without adversity?

For me, the most rewarding experience in my life has been being a parent. After my wife left me, I was left to raise my daughter, Linda, as a single dad. Having to do that was one of the toughest things I've ever done, and I freely admit that, like every parent, I made most of it up as I went along. I made a lot of mistakes, but I also got a few things right. I love my daughter, she loves me, and I am as proud of her as any man could ever be of his child. She is quite a lady and has a very promising life ahead of her.

I wouldn't trade that experience for anything. I think I learned twice as much from her as she learned from me, and it was worth every minute.

Event: _____

Lesson: _____

_____

_____

_____

_____

_____

# What Are Your Strengths?

In the blanks on the next page, I want you to write some of your greatest strengths. Really. You have them; you know what they are. I can hear you thinking, "I don't have any strengths. I don't know what to write." Again, I'm not really here and I can't see you or what you're writing, so you don't need to be modest. Just write down the things you're good at, your special qualities.

Think about it hard for a moment before you answer. Write down the things you truly do well, character traits you possess, resources at your command that will help you achieve your dream. You'll be calling on these resources time and time again, so write them down! Get reacquainted with them.

One of my greatest abilities is that I've always been able to move people to do things. I am a take-charge kind of guy, and groups tend to follow me when I come up with ideas, make suggestions, or give orders. I can get people to follow me, because I believe in what I'm saying and doing. I truly like people, and I think they can sense that I am earnest and sincere, and that I care about them.

## My first strength would be:

Lin: I am a strong leader. *And now it's your turn.*

You: _____

As a leader, I have always been able to catch the ear of my superiors and also impress my subordinates to imitate me.

## My second strength is:

Lin: A unique ability to motivate and influence others.

You: _____

Being a parent has taught me a lot. I'm not sure what I would have done without my daughter. She has turned out wonderfully—she isn't me and I don't always like everything she does, but she has a lot of my traits. The good ones, hopefully.

## My third strength is:

Lin: I am a loving father to my daughter.

You: _____

My life hasn't been any easier than the next guy's. In fact, it's been harder than average in many ways, but I try to never succumb to depression. Through all the times I've been down, whether I was thrown there, or fell there myself, so far I've always been able to pick myself up more times than I've fallen—though some occasions, such as my divorce, were very hard. I hope I will always have that as part of my personality.

## My fourth strength is:

Lin: I have the ability to bounce back from adversity.

You: _____

Through all three careers I've had—army officer, state employee, and motivational speaker—I've always had the opportunity to work with people of diverse backgrounds, people who were different from myself. In doing that, I have learned to relate to many people from different socioeconomic backgrounds, different races, different creeds and religions, different orientations and sexes.

I've been blessed with the gift of being able to help one side see the other side's point of view, which has allowed me to help all sorts of people learn to work together and even to understand and appreciate one another for their differences, as well as their similarities. This is one of my greatest gifts, and I thank God for it every day.

**My fifth strength would be:**
Lin: I have an ability to bridge the gap between people of diverse backgrounds and beliefs.

You: _____

# What Are Your Two Greatest Weaknesses?

Okay, you've come a long way. You've truthfully answered some tough questions. Now we're going to kick it up a notch, and get a little tougher before we're through. I'm going to ask you that question you've probably heard at every job interview you've ever had.

At the job interviews, though, you've most likely picked things like, "I care too much," or "I work too hard," so you can put a positive spin on any weakness you may have. You don't get to do that here. I want your two *real* weaknesses. And just to show you good faith, like I have all along, I'm going to tell you mine.

First, I have a hard time saying, "No" to people I like and respect, and because of that, I have a lot of things—too many things—going on in my life. More than I have time for. And it sometimes keeps me from committing the time I should to my goals and dreams. It has held me back on more than one occasion.

**My first weakness is:**

Lin: I have a hard time saying "no" when asked to do something by someone I like, so I tend to overextend myself.

You: _____

_____

_____

Second, my desire to help people occasionally becomes a liability. When I run into people that refuse to help themselves, sometimes, before I realize what I'm doing, I try too hard to help them. I forget the old saying about leading a horse to water. I really wish sometimes that I could make them drink.

**My second weakness is:**

Lin: I really want to help people, even sometimes those who do not want to help themselves, and it can use up a lot of my time as well as theirs.

You: _____

_____

# What Qualities Do You Want to Possess?

Okay, that was great, and you did a good job if you were honest in your answers. Hopefully, you're learning things you never knew about yourself, or maybe just never admitted.

But we're still not done. There's one more step before we move on. There are qualities that successful people have that you may wish you could have, too. And you *can* have them. For some of them, you'll need to be around people who are doing what you want to do. They will inspire and encourage you. Don't be surprised; some of them will even help you, coach you, and share in your dreams. They know what it takes to get there.

So what I want you to do now is list five qualities you *don't* have that you *want*. I'll give you examples by sharing some of mine.

1. Communication skills. I struggle with my writing, spelling, and speaking skills. I did not get the basics in school.
2. Shrewd judgment of the character of others. I want to learn to recognize better that people have to be willing to help themselves before I can help them to success.
3. Tolerance. I want to learn to accept that some people are happy being followers.
4. Patience. I want to develop a level of patience in dealing with others and to realize that their goals and timeline may not be the same as mine.
5. A carefree attitude. I want to develop the attitude that things truly are going to turn out for the best.

Now, it's your turn: *What are some qualities you wish you had?*

1. _____

   _____

2. _____

   _____

3. _____

   _____

4. _____

   _____

5. _____

   _____

The qualities you've listed can be learned or adopted. If you want them, you need to assume them, take them upon yourself, and they will become part of who you are, as automatic to you as breathing. Once you've developed the qualities you need, you'll be on your way, and success will show up precisely on time.

And there you have it. I've talked you through some tough questions, and I've shared with you some tough things about my own life, so you can see I wasn't born with a silver spoon and that things did not always come easily to me. The honest answers you've written down will be invaluable to you in learning to define and achieve your goals and dreams. I want you to go back through each one and see what you can learn about yourself.

After you've done that, then you'll be ready to proceed. I want you to keep this chapter in mind as you go on.

# 4 | No Man's Land: Faith versus Fear

*I can accept failure. Everyone fails at something. But I can't accept not trying.*

—Michael Jordan

*What would you attempt to do if you knew you could not fail?*

—Robert Schuller

---

So far, we've talked about your dreams, your goals, and what qualities you bring to the table in order to accomplish them. By now, hopefully, you'll have decided—or are getting very close to deciding—what your dream is, what your strengths are, and what you must do to get to where you want to be.

That's a great start on your way to success. And now that you're focused on your goal, consider the following:

When you know what you want to do, you must be prepared to make a commitment.

When you make that commitment, you've walked into what I call "No Man's Land." It's a dangerous and critical time for you and your dream. You've entered a realm where you will face roadblocks and setbacks, and it's crucial how you handle those. This is the critical make-you-or-break-you part of your journey.

Here in No Man's Land, something or someone is going to show up and test your resolve in what you want to do, and you have to be truly careful. This is the time when some people give in and say, "I don't have what it takes to do this." Fear will creep in the early mornings and late in the night, and it will ask: "Who are you? Why do you think you can write a book/sing professionally/change your career/ do what you love? What makes you special?"

Remember, this is something you *choose:* to step forward with resolve, or to run away.

# It Won't Be Easy

I began this book with a strong desire to tell each of you that if you follow the principles and steps laid out in this book, develop a high level of courage, passion, and self-confidence, and follow through to the end, you will achieve greatness in whatever you choose to do. But success isn't guaranteed.

There are many reasons some of you will fail. Some things are out of your control; for instance, a downward trend in the marketplace can be devastating to any newcomer. A partner may make a mistake. A death or an illness in the family may derail your dreams, at least for now. However, when everything is said and done, the major reason for failure lies within us. Wait! Don't turn me off or lay the book aside now.

Listen: *What I'm telling you is, we don't always make it on our first, second, or third try.* I personally don't know of anyone who hasn't faced some measure of failure before going on to succeed. Remember when I told you life is not easy? Well, success is not easy, either. Far from it.

So what is my point?

Everyone fails sometimes. How you respond to that failure is what makes or breaks you. To succeed, you have to get back in the ring. Look for other ways to accomplish your goals. Learn from your mistakes and try again: *Change your strategy or change your goals. Follow through. Don't quit.*

I can tell you firsthand, nothing is more humbling than failure at something you truly want to do. Yet even if you fail, what you take away from the experience can't be bought, and it is one of the things that can make you more determined to succeed.

In this chapter I will tell you my personal experience, how I rebuilt my life not once, but three times.

Once, when I was in the army, I was told that if I could hold my present pace and performance, there was a great possibility that I could make the rank of brigadier general—a lofty goal.

I received my commission without a degree and spent nine years in the enlisted ranks. Things seemed to be going my way, and I felt I was on top of my act, ready for the big time. My record exhibited the traits of a model soldier.

Then two things happened. My relationship with my wife began to get off track, and I didn't know how to get it back on. And at about the same time, I started to try to manage my own assignments. I was not equipped to handle either one, my marriage or my assignments. I needed help.

The army chose me to go to South Korea, with a return assignment to Fort Campbell, Kentucky, with a unit I served in while in Vietnam. For an infantry officer, this was a perfect route to success, and had I left it alone, who knows where I would be today.

However, I pulled some strings to get my assignment changed to Central America. Don't get me wrong; it was a good assignment. However, I was trying to save my marriage, which was going down fast.

Simply put, I failed in both of my goals.

Not only did my marriage end despite my efforts, but my assignment change ultimately led me to lose my career and any opportunity to rise to the rank of general.

Did it hurt? Of course. Failure always hurts. But if you maintain the proper attitude, difficult times will never leave you where they find you. They either leave you a better person or a more negative one. It's up to you. For me, it was not the end but the beginning. Did I try to blame someone else for my failure? No, not at all. Who was there to blame? It was my choice, my decision. I chose my path, and I lost. There was no one to blame but myself. I simply had too many balls in the air.

I took the responsibility for what happened to me. I sharpened my vision. I took these lessons hard, but I took them well. I reevaluated my desires, my goals, and dreams, and renewed my determination to become somebody and to do something I loved to do. I got back into the race of life.

I had to start all over again.

You have to remind yourself it's okay to lose sometimes, to start all over again, to stop and ask for directions from those who know more than you do. It's crucial that you get back up and try again. Truly, you have not lost or quit until you tell yourself you have.

If you want to succeed, it's essential to keep going.

All of the tasks, jobs, or opportunities I ever tried in my life started out being tough and difficult, as though they were a test I had to pass. It is the testing phase that determines how much we really want something. You have to see if it's going to work, and if it's not, you have to figure out how to make it. The only way you can do that is by testing your plan, stepping into the arena, and seeing what happens.

I think our fortunes can work in cycles. For instance, during my first five years in real estate, I made no profits whatsoever. My plan in the beginning was to purchase ten pieces of property with a net worth of $100,000 each. That would be my first million. But there I was, stretching my paycheck month to month just to make ends meet. At times during those five years, I was afraid to answer my phone for fear it would be one of my tenants calling with some wiring or plumbing problem that would cost me money that I didn't have.

But I hung in there. I stuck to my basic plan. By the time I turned sixty-five, I'd have a half million in cash and more than a million in assets. But it was not until the fifth year that things turned around for me. In the eighth year, I had caught the swing of things—the cycle had come around. I am convinced my plan was working. Today I am making money. I am realizing my goals.

You can achieve happiness, peace, and tranquility in your life and the lives of the people around you. Keep things simple. Be prepared for the difficult and disappointing times that come into your life. No matter how hard you work at making things right, things do go wrong, and sometimes, your support base will disappear when you most need it. Sometimes life throws you a fastball. Sometimes you strike out.

But that does not have to be the end.

Realize your goals. Start now. Read this book, make your plan, and then work your plan so it will work for you.

Will it be easy? No, no, *no.*

Did *I* want to quit? Yes. *Yes.* Several times.

But did I quit?

No.

There are no free lunches. Only a lot of hard work, attention to detail, and keeping your mind on the goal. Your plan will work only if you are willing to work it.

You know what you have to do: *Do it.*

It worked for me.

# Maintaining Your Drive

Many years ago, I was a drill instructor at Fort Leonard Wood, Missouri. In those days, once you hit a certain rank as an enlisted soldier, you became a noncommissioned officer (NCO). I was an NCO, and that was good, but one day I realized that I wanted something more out of life. I realized that day that I wanted to be a commissioned officer. I knew it would take a huge load of work on my part, because I was not prepared. But I thought a lot about it and decided it was what I wanted to do.

I made the commitment.

One day, as sergeants often do, I had to dress down a private who had messed up. He did something—I don't remember what— to merit a lecture, and I had to get in his face a little bit.

A particular second lieutenant (a commissioned officer) overheard me talking to the young man. Now, this officer thought a lot of the private in question, and he wasn't too happy about it.

He walked over to me, stuck his finger in my face, and said some pretty harsh things to me. He told me I was a temporary fix during a war, that I didn't have what it takes to make it as a career officer, and as soon as the war ended, the army would be rid of me, but that he and the private would still be there long after I was gone.

Clearly, the man wanted me to back down, but all he did was infuriate me. Instead of making me want to back down, he stiffened my resolve to meet the challenge I set for myself. It was he who helped sharpen my determination. Little does he know, I am forever grateful to him. Not because he did anything directly good for me, but because by trying to tell me what I could not do, he issued a challenge I swore I would meet.

I promised myself I would take the exam and pass it. I would become a commissioned officer in the U.S. Army. I would prove to myself that that man's prediction would fail, and that I would succeed—and I swore I would not only succeed, but also become an outstanding officer. And I did it.

The day I made that decision, I immediately showed my commitment by taking my first step into dangerous territory. And though they didn't do it intentionally, all my army buddies came to me one by one and tested my resolve. Once they heard about my goal, every single one of them asked me: "Are you crazy?" They told me I could be a sergeant major, which would put me among the top-ranking NCOs in the army—the most powerful of the enlisted men. They were amazed that I would want to jeopardize that chance by trying to become an officer, especially during wartime and without a college degree.

But think about it. If I stayed where I was, I would have retired a sergeant major instead of a lieutenant colonel.

No Man's Land. Folks started to laugh, wondering why I would want to take the risk and become a "freshman" again. My resolve began to waver. I began to think: "Lin, you do not have a college degree. Look at your competition."

But I'd made a commitment, and I stuck it out. I knew I didn't need to see around the corner. I was ready for this, committed to it, and knew I could succeed if I stayed on course. I knew if I stepped out in faith, the rest would be taken care of.

I had a desire to become an officer, and that second lieutenant—the lowest officer on the officer's totem pole—stuck his finger in my face. This single event was what kept me going. Every time I felt like quitting, I'd remember his finger in my face and I'd smile to myself. It made me more determined to succeed.

I took the test and applied for Officer Candidate School (OCS).

I waited for the answer, and while I waited, the others continued to laugh. It was difficult, but I made it through. I took it one step at a time, and I didn't quit. And guess what? I passed the test—

both the physical and oral boards.

I made it through and I was accepted.

Accepted! I couldn't believe it.

But here's the kicker: *I didn't make it.* Before they cut the orders, I went to Post Headquarters and withdrew my application.

Why?

The answer is simple: *fear.*

My friends—the people I thought would cheer me on—had been negative, and that had gotten to me. The people you associate with sometimes can cause you to doubt yourself. What they say will make you think about the things you can't do instead of the things you can. When you're climbing that rope, working your heart out to get to that point where you can say, "You know, I really think I can do this," somebody might shout: "Hey, don't look down!"

And what do you do?

You look down.

And when you look, you take your eyes off your prize, your mind leaves what you want and refocuses on the distance behind you instead of the distance you've got to go. You start thinking about things that can limit you instead of the wonderful possibilities of achieving your goal.

And you lose resolve. You lose desire. You lose that hanging power and stick-to-itiveness.

And you start questioning yourself. You become afraid, and if you don't realize what's happening, this is probably where you'll quit. Remember, "obstacles are the things you see when you take your eyes off your goal."

Fear, unchecked, is like nerve gas to our dreams.

Nerve gas is usually invisible, odorless. You can't see, feel, or touch it. But it's there. And once it gets to your system, it's devastating. It can kill you in seconds, and it's one of the most violent, painful deaths imaginable.

This is what fear does.

Fear will blind you. Have you ever been in a cave where you cannot see your hand in front of your face? Try it. Go into a basement room and turn out all the lights. Try to move around. This is what fear does to you.

We could talk about how fear makes our hearts beat faster or our palms sweat. But the biggest thing fear does is it prevents people from achieving their objectives, from moving forward and living their dreams. For you to be able to do that, you must learn to overcome fear.

There's an old saying "a coward dies a thousand deaths." I withdrew my application for OCS—which was one act. But well before I did that, I had withdrawn it a hundred times in my mind. My friends told me I might not make it. In the No Man's Land, I had started to doubt myself. I believed my friends and let the nerve gas of fear creep in and destroy my desires.

But then, when you forgo an opportunity, you will relive it every day for the rest of your life. When you withdraw your own applications—letting little doubts and fears about the future and change come in—how many times does that play in your mind?

That's when the "shoulda beens" come into your head at three o'clock in the morning, like nerve gas, and play like a movie—over and over again.

Fear will tie you up like a straitjacket. It will cause you to turn and run when nobody's chasing you.

Someone you know will question your dream—tell you "you can't," "you shouldn't," or "you don't need to." They will honestly believe they're doing you a favor.

But they don't understand the agony in your heart when you report every day to a job doing something you don't like to do.

There are far more people in the world doing something they don't like than there are people who are. But take heart: There are folks who are doing what they love and loving what they do. Every day is a "road trip" to them, and they allow themselves to see the positive things in life. They see the colors in life. You can be like them.

Fear has caused more people to turn back than any other reason for failure. Be prepared for it. It is something that you must overcome if you hope to see success.

A friend of mine, Maureen, lost her husband, job, home, and car, and still had it inside her to keep going and rebuild her life. I remember seeing her fight back the tears because she didn't have a "worthy" job and could not pay the bills. I would sit with her and encourage her, because I saw something in her: She was a *fighter*. I watched her struggle, stretch, cry, and beg, but she had the guts to pull herself up from having practically nothing to acquiring a sales job that earns her more than $60,000 a year. She fought for it; she would not be denied her rightful place at the table.

How could she go so far? Why didn't she stop at $30,000? More than one person has told me that the loss of material things is "freeing." They ask me, rhetorically, "What is it that keeps people chained and locked to material *things?*" Why are so many people stuck working at jobs they hate and with people they don't like?

Fear creeps in like nerve gas and conditions us not to risk or stretch or desire more. It is this conditioning that forces us to remain in one place.

Fleas can be conditioned in this way. Anyone who's owned a dog knows that fleas have the ability to jump quite high. But if you trap fleas in a cardboard box with a top, the fleas will jump up and hit the top of the box repeatedly. It's not too long, however, until they are no longer jumping high enough to hit the top.

But the story goes on: If you open the box, the fleas continue to jump, but they can't jump out of the box.

Why? It's very simple: The fleas have become conditioned to not jump any higher than the limits they've been taught.

This is why we have so many people, of all colors and walks of life, saying "I can't. They won't let me." Why do you think welfare families remain poor through three and four generations? Is it possible they've become conditioned to accept only what they are given, to never want to be more than what they are?

On some level, we all do the same thing. Someone says to himself, "I'm probably not going to get that job." He interviews well, but nobody calls. The end of the week comes, and next week comes, and he sits there, still waiting.

So he screws down his courage and goes out for a second interview, and a third.

Now he's reached the point where questions begin to creep in like nerve gas.

When this fellow doesn't get the job, he may say, "I can't jump out of this situation because they won't let me. They won't let me get what I deserve; they want to keep me where I am; they don't want me to succeed."

The truth is, at this point he's conditioned to stay where he is, so he has to look for reasons why he isn't making progress.

He gets lost in the No Man's Land.

Michael Jordan once said that as a young man, he'd be out in front of the gym at six, waiting for its doors to open. That attitude took him to great heights.

Tiger Woods said that he used to wait for the sun to come up so he could practice. And when the weather was bad, he'd practice inside. Look where he is today.

But it didn't happen for either of them immediately, either. They each went through the No Man's Land. When the things we want don't happen immediately, we have to remember that this doesn't mean we missed the target. It just means we are *afraid* our desires won't be fulfilled. We've conditioned ourselves to stay where we're at, and we make excuses.

—"I'm not good enough."
—"I have to take care of the kids."
—"It's a pipe dream. Nothing like that will happen to me."

Charles Lindbergh once said, "What kind of a person would live in a world where there is no daring?" Dare. Try. Keep going. This kind of determination moves you away from fear, and it moves you toward your dream. Keep daring, keep on your path, and at some point, when the time is right, when you least expect it, you will reach your destination. You will step into the circle of success, and fear will have no place in your life.

# Self-Talk

Self-talk is helpful, if we can remember that we need to keep it positive. We all have something in this world that we would love to do. In our heads, we often draw a distinction between thinking and talking about it, and really taking action. You may be thinking—telling yourself—that it is impossible to live your dream. But just remember that you will act on what you think about the most. If you think that your dream, purpose, or calling is impossible, impractical, and out of your reach, make no mistake about it: this is what you will act out. It is far better to keep your thoughts—your "self-talk"—positive, than to set up a self-fulfilling negative prophecy. Keep it positive! Tell yourself, "Yes, I can!"

# The Rest of the Story

Well, I didn't let fear get to me too long. Eighteen months after I removed my application for Officer Candidate School, I resubmitted it. And this time, on the advice of my colonel, I went to Fort Benning to learn to become an officer.

But was I out of the woods? No.

During the Vietnam conflict, they accepted me as an officer—a second lieutenant, as fate would have it—because they needed officers. They needed this kind of "Christmas Help" (as they called us) because the war was so spread out, so soldiers became officers overnight. I knew if I didn't do something to make myself an exceptional officer, an outstanding performer, I would get caught up in the reduction that was bound to happen after the war.

I knew that only four things would ensure my remaining an officer after the war: education, performance, determination, and taking responsibility for myself.

So I studied in the evenings and on weekends for a long time. It seemed an eternity of working during the day, going home and studying, and going to class while everyone else watched TV, went to ballgames, had barbecues in their backyard, and slept.

And I got my degree.

As the years went by, I got a promotion. And another. And another. Most of my promotions came ahead of those of my contemporaries, and I retired from the U.S. Army a lieutenant colonel, some twenty years after that lowly second lieutenant stuck his finger in my face and told me I didn't have what it takes.

# Faith

Most people today, as Thoreau wrote, "lead lives of quiet desperation." Not many of us manage to move from where we are and climb the ladder to where we want to be. The rest continue to live their quiet lives of desperation.

Why do so many folks stay in abusive relationships, jobs that they're unhappy with, schools or degree programs they hate, failing marriages? Well, as we said, they find excuses, but the bottom line is this: Everything we do, we do for one of two reasons. The first is the promise of reward; the second is the fear of punishment.

Think about it—why do you perform your job well? Certainly you have a work ethic, but is the underlying reason that there is always a promise of a raise, attention, promotion? And for some people, the work ethic itself is little more than feeling good about yourself because you did something correctly.

Am I right?

And what about when we don't do what we know we should?

Fear: It's all out of fear of failure, criticism, anger—what other people will think. Or perhaps we fear even worse things. We could be fired. A spouse may beat us. Someone may threaten us.

But it always boils down to fear, the nerve gas of our dreams.

So how do we live with fear? There is a way.

When I left the army, I was scared, nervous, and stressed out. The thing I was afraid of was change. You see, fear can paralyze you. It can stop you in your tracks.

After spending thirty years in the army—two of those years in combat—one would think that I would have conquered fear.

But I had not. Very few people do.

Fear is always lurking in the corners of our mind, taking different forms, waiting like an enemy to ambush you when you least expect it. You have to deal with fear, because it jeopardizes your attitude and your passion for what you want.

The way to deal with fear is with faith and grace. There is no substitute for knowing what you want, and for having the faith, belief, courage, and guts to go for your dreams. If you believe in what you want, create a vision of it, and stay focused on it, your opportunities will show up precisely on time.

Faith is the opposite of fear. The two cannot coexist for long in the same environment; one or the other will soon dominate. When you recognize fear's presence, feel it, but don't let it shake your faith.

Overcoming fear takes courage, endurance, and plain old guts. Each one of these is a learned habit, and if it's a learned habit, you can develop it yourself.

To increase your faith, you have to overcome your doubts. Overcome your doubts by focusing on something bigger than you. For me it was my belief in God.

Sometimes we are in circumstances or situations that are hard to overcome. Sometimes things go bad in our lives. Then fear starts dominating our thought process, and at that point it can influence how we react to the situation. The negative comes out. We start blaming others for our situation, and before long, we begin to think about giving up, and we start thinking negative thoughts like "What's the use?" "Nothing good ever happens to me." And "I knew it would turn out this way."

When you were standing around thinking about it, you had the courage, but once you actually got to the doing, you fell away.

If this happens to you, you haven't made the commitment. You're playing with faith. You have to *make* the commitment and tell people what your dreams and goals are. Tell everyone you see. Doing that, you will reinforce in yourself the commitment, and you will make people ask you why.

At this stage, you don't have to know why. You just need to know that you have the commitment and vision, and that everything you do should be committed to that dream.

Les Brown once said, "If you get up every morning acting like what you want to be, then soon you will become what you act like." Act like what you want to be, and soon you will become that—it's not a lie, but a statement of faith.

If you want to overcome fear, you have to be able to say to yourself, "I can run faster with one hundred people that want to go than I can with one who wants to stay put."

Remember the difference between a hero and coward? They are the same, except that the coward stays in the foxhole, and the hero steps out.

Once you have made the commitment, you have to hold the vision. And whatever vision you hold in front of you—take the steps toward achieving your goal. Just realize that if you let fear creep in like nerve gas, you could lose that vision.

That's where faith comes in: You overcome your fears by increasing your faith.

---

*Let's review:* you've done the research on your life, and you've come face-to-face with what you need to do. You've made the commitment, but now you're in the No Man's Land wondering what to do.

Take the next step. You know what it is. Look for that new job. Practice your singing. Keep working on those speeches. Whatever. Just do it, and the rest will come.

It's called faith. Someone once said, "I don't need to see around the corner, I just need to trust Him and take the next step."

That's faith.

But I want to make extra sure you know what I'm talking about. What is faith?

When I talk about faith, I mean several things. The more kinds of faith you have on your side, the more equipped you'll be to deal with any fear that creeps into your mind.

The first kind of faith I'm talking about is faith in yourself. You've made a decision, a commitment. You must *know* that within yourself you have the courage, the strength, the intestinal fortitude that it takes to see things through, no matter what anybody says. It took a lot for me to go and put in that second application for OCS, and it took a lot of effort to complete my classes and training. It wasn't easy, but I stuck to it, and I pat myself on the back every time I remember that I did it.

The second kind of faith is faith in some kind of Higher Power. Speaking for myself, I am God-centered. I don't mean to insist that you should share any of the particulars of my Christian beliefs, but I'm certain that part of the reason I've been successful is my faith in a supreme being that coordinates things. You can call on this Power or Spirit, too, whether you believe it to be the Christian or Jewish

God, Allah, the wisdom of the Buddha, the nature gods of paganism, or simply a "Something out There," a Universal Force, that takes care of things for you. Having a spiritual belief can help quite a bit in times of crisis; keep this in mind as you follow your path.

Third, I'm talking about a more generic kind of faith: the simple trust that things will always work out for the best—and if you can develop your plan and work toward achieving your goals, they always do.

# Faith Can Give You Motivation

Faith is the untouchable thing that makes a guy sign up for Officer Candidate School when everyone else says he shouldn't.

It's that thing that makes a woman quit her job and travel to Los Angeles in hopes that she can meet an agent and become an actress or model.

It's that thing that gets you through when everyone else says no; it's that mysterious force that guides you through to the other side of No Man's Land.

It's related to courage, but it's not the same thing. Faith creates courage, creates motivation. Faith is that thing that gets the hero out of the foxhole when the grenades are flying. The faith that he'll accomplish his mission, whether he gets killed or not.

It's a sense of something higher. A sense of something higher is what's going to get you out of the No Man's Land.

An event that was really tough for me was my first airborne jump, which I've already talked a little bit about. Looking back it was fun, and I had the courage to do it. It didn't hurt or kill me, and it was something I really wanted to do. Over the jump zone, the green light came on.

And I had a decision to make.

Do I jump, or run? Could you do it? You get to the door, and you're told to jump; you're fourteen thousand feet above the ground, and the jumpmaster says "Go." Fear taps on your shoulder and says, "Hey, you could die."

But you know what? At that point, faith kicks in and says, "You've done this dozens of times forty feet above the ground, and you hopped out with no fear every time the jumpmaster told you to go. So you can do it now."

I had faith that day, and I was the first out the door. I jumped, landed, and walked off the field. It was a perfect jump.

It's always good when you hit the ground in a successful jump and you feel good about yourself.

But you're not finished. You don't get your *wings* until that fifth jump. What sends you up those four more times? Is it faith or is it fear?

The answer is obvious. Fear keeps you on the ground, and you quit! Fear keeps you in the foxhole. Fear keeps you from doing what it takes to achieve our goals and live your dreams.

Martin Luther King Jr. didn't quit when it came time to go back to Memphis. He had known he was the target for an assassin's gun for quite some time. He knew he probably wouldn't live to see the promised land of full Civil Rights, but what made him continue?

In exactly the same way that King went to Memphis and Lin Appling jumped out of a perfectly good airplane, it's no different, no matter what your dream is—whether you want to be an actor, be a singer, own your own business, or whatever. Things don't come naturally; you have to work at them, and have faith.

Faith also works when you've messed up, when life has thrown you curve balls. What causes someone to get back up to bat when he made a sorry performance the day before?

What causes a person to love again after a messy divorce?

What causes a person to drive again after a nasty accident?

The bottom line is that fear and faith cannot coexist in the same room, cannot coexist in the same place, cannot coexist in the same mind. If you are truly committed to something, faith will help you to accomplish it.

You face your fear straight on and go through No Man's Land. That's what makes heroes. That's what helps us achieve our dreams. Fear holds you back; faith moves you forward.

You will find that if you exercise faith—faith in yourself, faith in God, and the simple faith that things will work out fine—and if you show your commitment by stepping forward, fear slips quietly out the back door.

# A Final Thought

What, then, is your driving force? Is it faith, or is it fear?

Fear will keep you frozen in your tracks, unmoving, unchanging, and unachieving.

Faith will motivate you to begin your path to success and it will empower you to proceed the full distance to reach your goal. Whatever it is that you want, *faith is how you get there.*

# 5 | Making the Change: A Significant Emotional Event

*The future belongs to those who believe
in the beauty of their dreams.*

—Eleanor Roosevelt

This chapter is about change; specifically, a change in the direction of your life. In the first four chapters we talked about identifying your goal, recognizing what you bring to the table, and being prepared to deal with fear. Now we are going to look at changes that happen within yourself, change that is brought on by adversity, hardship, and significant emotional events.

Are you suffering from hardship? Have you recently lost your job? Are you facing or emerging from a divorce—or any other kind of loss? Are you struggling just to pay your bills and make ends meet? Have you been told that you will be laid off? Have you been told that you have a serious medical condition? If so, then you need to read on, because thousands of people have traveled this road before you and come out victorious.

When people feel the pain of devastating loss, they quite often come back with a desire to succeed that's stronger than ever. Losing something so important has a very sobering and humbling effect. There is an old saying, "sometimes you have to get fired before you get fired up." Remember, I have been fired twice in my life, I quit the highest-paying job that I had ever held up to that point, and I lived through an excruciating divorce. At times of significant emotional loss, when we're at our lowest, it is time to become absolutely clear of our goals. Self-delusion is at a minimum; we have nowhere to go but up—so we might as well choose the path to happiness and success.

Let me ask you again: What do you really, really want? Do you know? As we've already noted, getting a clear picture of what you want to do with the rest of your life is not as easy as one might think. Finding your lifelong desires while bouncing back from a tragedy in life is difficult at best. Especially in a country where there are so many possibilities from which to choose. Sometimes it becomes too painful to decide what we truly want, so we settle for the belief that we can never have it. At that point, it seems much easier to quit and settle for whatever floats downstream. My advice to you is to not get caught up in that pattern of belief. During my lifetime, and almost without exception, in my observations of every successful person's life, I've noted that life is filled with examples of rejection, failure, disappointment, letdowns, delays, setbacks, hardships, and obstacles to overcome. You have to develop the attitude that even if tragedy lurks around the corner, you will simply keep believing in your goals, keep moving, have faith, and be willing to change.

Starting over can be one of the most difficult and stressful events in a person's life. People do it every day: A man quits his stable job and moves to New York to pursue acting; a woman leaves her husband of twenty-five years and moves to Colorado to teach school; another friend gives up a promising position in a company to start a creative freelance career. It must feel like jumping out of an airplane. Why take such risks?

# Why Do People Do This?

Are you one of them? Have you experienced a personal tragedy, and if so, how can you get started on your new life? That is what happened to me. After my divorce, I was left to raise my daughter as a single parent; and I've been fired twice—a loss of employment is terrifying! In 1985 I lost everything that I had with the exception of my career and my daughter. I had to borrow the money to move from Florida to Missouri. Overwhelming? You bet! A wake-up call? You guessed it! It was an emotional event unlike anything I had ever experienced in my life. You see, two years in Vietnam was much easier to accept than the breakup of my family. When families break up and go separate ways, there are no "winners." The key to dealing with tragedy is not so much what happens to you, but how you handle it when it does happen.

Take it from me, you can bounce back. It's not at all easy, but when you're through with your initial shock and grieving, you've got to get back into life again, or you could become trapped sitting in a corner, sucking your thumb, saying "nobody loves me" or "nobody cares." You see, no matter how innocent you feel, or how hopeless you perceive your situation—if you don't stand up and start doing something, you'll be stuck in your tragedy. There is a time to moan, and then it's time to move on. There is no getting "over" it—you have to get *through* it. Yes, it's painful, but you can do it!

That's what this book is all about—learning to embrace change. Every day, thousands of people change their lives. So can you. You can start over, you can make a change, and you can learn how to discover what you want to do and how to go about doing it. It's inside you. All you have to do is figure it out and take the necessary steps to get there. You may have doubts; we all do. Your most valuable resource is you.

If you are waiting for the right moment, you will likely *never* get it done. Just get started—the right time is now, and there are people that really do care and will help you! If you have the courage to ask

# Why Do People Start Over?

What causes a person to pick up from Georgia and move across the country to Los Angeles without a clue of what he's going to do, carrying with him only his dreams, and weather the storm of life, the setbacks, the disappointments, the *no*s? What causes him to stay true to his dream and go on to find happiness, an enjoyable life, become a true success? What keeps him there, doing what he loves and loving what he does?

The catalyst is almost always a significant emotional event that brings disruption and change. It sounds bad, doesn't it? It might be painful, but it's not entirely bad. Sometimes it turns into a good thing.

It's just that we can't see it at the time.

It usually starts when you realize that you're simply not getting what you know you should be getting or that you have decided you want.

You are the person who has to make this judgment: Does your current life make you happy? Does it give you the satisfaction you need, whether it be financial, emotional, professional, spiritual, or physical?

*At this point, ask yourself:*
1. Who am I?
2. What do I want?
3. What am I afraid of? (this is a key question, please don't skip it)
4. Who do I most admire, and why?
5. What tasks have brought me the most success?

And you may finally come to this realization: *You know that where you are is not where you want to be.*

You know that you can do something better with your life. You want to make your parents, your spouse, or your children proud. You want to travel. You want to get away from your present job or an abusive spouse or a relationship that is going nowhere. You want, you want, you want.

Until it finally happens—a sign. An emotional event that upsets the balance and accentuates the dissatisfaction in your life. Often when you're feeling pain, you know that you need to change.

The emotional event can take any form, and it's up to you how you react to it. The bottom line is, whatever happens, it makes you realize that you want more out of life, that you want to be happy, more fulfilled, whatever—you realize there is more out there than what is immediately around you.

The motivational speaker Les Brown tells a story about a young man who is walking along the street and sees an old man and his dog sitting on a porch. The dog is squirming, moaning, and obviously in pain.

The man is in a hurry, but his curiosity gets the better of him, and he asks the old man sitting nearby, "What's the matter with your dog?"

"He's lying on a nail," replies the old man.

"He's lying on a nail? That's all? Why doesn't he move?"

Says the old man, "He's not hurting bad enough."

That is to say, the dog's pain wasn't great enough to move—he had no motivation or catalyst to get him off that nail. The discomfort was building, but it hadn't reached that magical point yet. The behaviorists say that our brain responds to two stimuli—pain and pleasure, and until the pain outweighs the pleasure of our current situation, we will continue coasting on our inertia, not moving or growing, but simply existing. But when that point is reached, when the pain finally overpowers the pleasure, we will move.

We all have our nails, and we will all lie and squirm on them until the discomfort becomes pain, the pain becomes agony, and the agony becomes torture. At that point, and only at that point, will we encounter our catalyst, our trigger, and get off that nail, move to action, and make the change.

The catalyst can be literally anything. Anything. A dream, a random thought, a song, a conversation, a movie, or seeing tragedy in someone else's life. Then, the desire to do something in your life becomes so strong it cannot be denied. But these catalysts often fit into one of the following categories.

---

Some people wake up and find they are not passionate about what they do. Perhaps they were once, and the magic has faded, or perhaps they never were. But the day comes, at work, at home, in the car, and they realize they're not happy—not passionate about doing what they do, not passionate about how they're doing it, and not passionate about the people they're doing it with.

They've spent such a long time going through the motions, and one day the realization comes to them—often through an emotional event—they are dying on the vine. Some people just have to get away from the boredom and pain of what they're doing and how they're living.

Some people dream to be free of whatever chains them down. Do you have a dream? Of course you do—we all do. This book is part of mine. Something you've always wanted to do: travel, start a business, spend more time with your family, learn to paint, or find a way to help others.

Sometimes people who are successful executives, senior staff, presidents, or CEOs realize that they are receiving no satisfaction from their jobs and quit. A year ago, one of my friends left a prestigious position in state government after having worked his way steadily up the ladder for seventeen years. But he yearned for new challenges and new ways to advance; now, he's pursuing opportunities in the private sector.

Sometimes the significant emotional event is felt by many. Think of New Yorkers after 9/11. After that trauma, the place where they've spent so much time no longer seems the same. For many, a pall settles over the city, and they say, "I can't do this. I can't stay here any more. I have to start over somewhere—do something different." In their case, the significant emotional event comes from without.

---

Some people simply desire something different. Something they want not because they need it, but because they simply want it. Sometimes what we want is just more free time—more time for ourselves, more time for pursuing dreams, more time for fun, more time for spending with their loved ones. And sometimes we crave a different view and a different lifestyle.

It happens every day. It could happen to you.

You just might be at that stage in your life right now.

Could I be right?

*Could it be you?*

# How Can I Start Over?

*There's a formula for making this happen for you:*

—Get clear on what it is you want or need;

—Take out the trash; and

—Design a strategy for getting there.

That's how simple it is. It's a basic process of getting from where you are to where you want to be.

**Get clear on what it is you want or need.** I know I'm repeating, but this is paramount. It could be as simple as quitting what you are doing right now. What do you love to do? What are you good at? What would put a smile on your face; make you glad to get up in the morning?

You have to make that decision. Come to a final understanding of what's missing in your life and what will fill it. What's your dream? What makes you happy? What is it that wakes you up in the middle of the night knowing you need to be doing it? What is it that breaks your heart when you see someone else doing it, and you know you could be doing it too, maybe better?

That's your goal. Once you've isolated it, you must center your thoughts on the fact that it is possible for you to achieve it. Remember, you become what you think about the most. Otherwise, what would all this be for? You can live your dreams. Believe you can. Know you can. Take it on. And you will.

*Have a clear vision of your desire.*

**Take out the trash.** In every such situation, there will be things that will hold you back, waste your time, divert your attention, and weigh you down. It's got to go. It's all got to go. Get rid of the baggage. Sometimes this "baggage" takes the form of a destructive emotional relationship. Sometimes it takes the form of the notorious "time-wasters" in our lives—people who take up our time needlessly or things you do that distract you from the prize. Reflect upon all the little things that waste your precious time: computer games, TV, drinking—sometimes it's the crossword puzzle. Compare what you gain from these activities to what you might gain by staying focused.

This can be the most difficult step. It can be so hard to say no to something, even when you know it's for the best. But cut it loose, just let it go. Make a choice between what you want, and the world of distractions out there that will keep you from what you want. Cut loose the excess baggage, scrape off the barnacles, take out the trash. Free yourself.

This is necessary before you can move forward.

*Let go of the things that are weighing you down, and stay focused.*

**Design a strategy for getting there.** This is just a matter of breaking up your big goal into a bunch of smaller ones that you can keep track of. If you want to learn to play the piano, you don't say, "Okay, I'm going to learn the piano today"—you have to *start* somewhere. First you have to find a piano to play. You have to buy or rent a piano— which sometimes requires some shopping around—or else you have to obtain permission to use a piano at church, at a school, or at a friend's house. Then you get lessons or buy a self-instruction manual. Then you go through your lessons step by step, one day at a time, and practice, practice, practice. You have a series of different things to do; you have to have a plan.

This is the perfect time for you to write down *your* plan. Make several steps that you can achieve and be proud of as you progress toward your goal. As you check items off your list, you'll feel a sense of satisfaction that will help you stay positive if you encounter any setbacks.

Plan your next moves: step 1, step 2, step 3 . . .

*Develop your strategy.*

There's one final thing I didn't mention before. This is the thing that will make it all possible for you.

You have to know in your heart that there is something better around the corner. You don't need to *see* around the corner, you just have to have the faith that something better is there. If you have a strong desire and the faith, you can do it.

Just take the first step, and don't look back.

# The Importance of Persistence

One more thing you need is persistence. You'll never get where you're going if you don't have a burning desire—a passion—and the persistence to reach that destination, accomplish that goal, and be somebody!

Anyone who has the guts to start over in any form, especially those who don't know what's going to happen, must have a certain amount of passion and persistence. These are characteristics that will drive you when you're ready, and only when you're ready. They give you the feeling that tells you that even though you don't know what's out there, you know you have to go. Desire pushes you into the road so that all you have to do is start walking. It's passion that gets you really fired up inside and compels you to make a positive change in your life.

Say what you're going to be, and as you do so, feel how strongly you want it. Your passion will get you going and your persistence will carry you forward. Notice your feelings as you answer these questions again:

—What do you want?
—What do you want your life to be like?
—What holds you back?

Answer those questions, take out the trash, and you will start to make that change. *Follow your instincts, pinpoint your passion, keep it simple, and don't run scared.*

# Ed and Margie Imo

"When my mother asked why I wanted to marry Ed Imo, I told her it was because he said, 'I'm going to *be somebody.'*" These are the words of Margie Imo, as she remembers her husband's early aspirations for going into the restaurant business. "He always said he was going to be somebody: 'maybe it'll be a little grocery business, but I'm going to be somebody.'"

Now that there are nearly a hundred Imo's Pizza restaurants in and around Missouri and he has a gorgeous house with a beautiful garden and a small pizzeria for entertaining friends and family in the backyard, one can definitely say Ed Imo has become somebody. When you drive through Missouri, keep an eye out for the green and red sign that says "Imo's"; below this sign you will discover some of the best pizza in the world.

But Ed Imo wasn't always a pizza magnate.

In fact, he started out his business life working for a contractor, specifically his older brother. His other brother, John, worked as a tile setter, and he was the "helper." The idea was that you began as a helper, then moved up to apprentice, and finally became a tile setter yourself.

"So at the time, I remember that John was making ten thousand dollars a year, and you know, that was pretty good for those days. But I was making eight thousand, and I said, 'I want to make two thousand more a year.' We thought if we could make ten thousand a year, we could buy a house."

In those days, an annual income of eight thousand dollars wasn't too bad, but it wasn't that great, either, so after marrying in 1961, Ed and Margie decided they wanted something more.

They spent a lot of time discussing how to get out of their apartment and into something more comfortable. Since their favorite food was pizza, they took a look at that market and came up with a plan.

In those days, no one delivered pizza. If anyone wanted pizza at home, they had to call in the order and then go to the restaurant to get it. Some restaurants had a place off to one side where customers could wait for their orders, but usually anyone who wanted pizza had to sit and wait in the restaurant. The Imos thought, "wouldn't it be neat if someone would bring it to us," much like the gentleman down the road who delivered chicken?

After that, things fell into place.

It took some time to save the fifteen hundred dollars they needed to get started, but once they did, they committed themselves. They found a restaurant space for the right price: forty dollars a month. They made just the pizzas they liked—with no secret ingredients, no special sauce—just the basics.

The family was against it. Ed's brothers wouldn't let him quit his day job, so when he finished his tiling work, he simply went to his other job, making pizzas at night.

At first, it was difficult. "You start off with fifteen dollars in change the first night of business, and the first week, at the end of the week, you get your money. Then the next week, when the supplies come, you pay that and put ten dollars away for rent for the week, and everything like that, and at the end of the week, if you have any extra, it was yours."

At no time did they ever consider quitting. They knew very early on they had a winner.

After a few months, it became clear that money could be made. They started working the pizza business full time, with Margie at the counter and Ed making pizza.

How did they do it? Perseverance. "You've got to have a passion for what you do," Ed and Margie told me over the table. "You just can't get up in the morning and not have the enthusiasm to get moving."

By sheer willingness to do what was necessary and sticking to that decision—that commitment—Ed and Margie and their family have succeeded in the restaurant trade, one of the most difficult ventures to succeed in. Now they have six children—Frank,

Vince, John, Carl, Carol, and Mary— along with fourteen grandchildren, all in the business, successfully combining family and work. And one of the main ingredients of their success was that they started with something they loved to do: make pizzas.

"We just use good ingredients, offer good service, and give the people what they want. You get out of your business what you put into it. If you work hard, you can make money and enjoy what you do."

Perseverance and commitment. They got out what they put in. They built more than success—they built great success. A hundred stores is no small accomplishment.

This is a family who did what they loved and fell in love with what they did. "It's so simple to make something successful," says Ed Imo. "Find a need and fill it. I think nowadays everyone seems to want to have someone else do things for them. But you have to be responsible for your own success."

# 6 | Hard Times: What Is Your Anchor?

*It's a funny thing about life; if you refuse to accept anything but the best, you very often get it.*

—W. Somerset Maugham

All of us have something that keeps us on course. Some of you may have lost track of what that is, but if you stop and think about it, you can find it again. What do you draw strength from? What is that Center in your life that makes things just a little easier? That force that you depend on when things become difficult? Where do you run when things get tough? Who do you call on?

The thing that answers these questions in your life is your anchor. It's what keeps you steady when it's stormy or you can't see where you're going. It's what keeps you safe. You have to believe in something bigger than yourself. Some people call this their Higher Power; some call it the Universe; some, like myself, call it God. Whatever you call it, this is the anchor that focuses your life and guides you to your goal.

If you're not spiritual, then your anchor might be a person, concept, or belief that you depend on. It could be someone you trust to be supportive and to provide that safety net when things get rough and you start to fall. It could be an ideology, notions of justice and human ethics, or a belief in the American way. Whatever this thing is, it is always within reach. It is something that will keep you holding on.

For some of you, it might be a sense of faith in yourself, the knowledge that you can get through the rough spots in your life, for it only takes sufficient courage, endurance, and guts. Yet without this sense of faith, it's just a matter of time before you let go.

Or it might be something completely different; a sense of oneness you feel when you're outdoors in nature, or an unshakable belief that you have a purpose in life.

Whatever this thing is, it makes you feel elevated—like you're standing at the top of a ladder or on a mountaintop and can easily see your way. Whatever reassures you, that's your anchor.

That anchor will give you that same feeling when you're adrift in the ocean and can't see the way home; with your anchor, you know there is a way.

You need to find your own anchor—everyone's is different. In this chapter, we'll gain an understanding of what your anchor is like and how and when it works for you.

# Standing Alone

There is some bad news before we go much further.

The difficulty with depending on other people is that you must be absolutely sure of them. And you will be as time goes by, one way or another. The question you need to ask yourself is, "Whom can I trust with my dream?"

As you start to pursue your dream, some of those folks you thought you could count on for help and support might start to fall away. Don't worry, this is natural. It happens to all of us when we start to pursue your dreams. Some of the folks who separate themselves from you won't worry you so much; they'll drop away simply because you no longer have the same interests, and that's to be expected and is perfectly okay. You will find new contacts and acquaintances with similar interests, and they will step forward to help you. Remember: "Hang around with the winners."

It may distress you to lose the support of other friends, however. These folks will actually get angry or upset; they may blame you for being "self-centered," "too good for us," or "off in your own little world." These sorts of folks are the ones who prevent us from achieving our dreams. The naysayers. There are all sorts of reasons why these people try to talk us out of working to get our hearts' desire, but one of the main ones is simple jealousy.

And these may be your closest friends, perhaps even members of your family. The folks you respect most and expected support from. But you cannot draw strength from naysayers. In fact, you will have to spend less time with them if you want to achieve your goals in life. They will drag you down.

Let me repeat that: *They will drag you down.*

Remember, if people cannot see hope for themselves, they cannot see it for you.

You're doing something they aren't doing and desperately want to do: You're going after your dream; you're reaching out to be somebody.

Don't point that out to them, however, because they probably don't realize they're holding you back. They probably believe they're preventing you from getting hurt, "reminding you of your responsibilities," or even "helping you keep your feet on the ground" (whatever that means).

You don't have to cut them loose forever. Just spend less time with them until you achieve what you want. Then they can say all they want and you can just sit back and smile. You will find that in the end they will say, "I knew you could do it. I knew all the time that you had it in you . . . Now, can you help me?" They will invariably ask you for help for themselves, their kids, or their brother-in-law.

But when you cut loose and actually look for your dream, look to achieve your goals, you will most likely have to stand alone, because many of our so-called friends will fall away. Who can blame them? By identifying and pursuing your dream, you remind them of their own doubts; at some level, your action serves as a wake-up call to them: they may realize that what they are doing is not their real dream, purpose, passion, or goal. So many of us settle for something less than what we can be. Why? Because we don't take the time to use our mind. Because we too often listen to other people telling us that there are thousands of people already out there doing what we want to do. Then we start to believe that there is no more room for us. Listen to me: I hope that you are ready to be challenged.

We live in a lonely and tough world. We have been very successful in making things bad. Yet the United States is the greatest country in the world (I believe that it is). We are extremely lucky to live here. It brings tears to my eyes when I hear Lee Greenwood sing the song

"God Bless the U.S.A.," or when I hear Ray Charles sing "America the Beautiful." We have precious freedoms here that too many of us take for granted. However, at the time I am writing this chapter, more than nine hundred thousand Americans have lost their jobs in the past two years. Overwhelming? Yes!

If by chance you are reading this book and you are one of those people, I don't need to ask you if you are facing tough times. Devastating? Yes! I can relate to that fear, that pain—remember, in 1991, I too lost my job. But I invite you to follow the path that I followed and bounce back. This is the "Possibility Thinking Path" that Dr. Robert H. Schuller wrote about in the early eighties in his book *Tough Times Never Last, but Tough People Do!* The title of that book says it all. When you go out tomorrow looking for a job—the opportunity to earn a living for yourself and your family—you need to keep in mind that *this will work out* if you trust the process. If you believe things will work out, they will. Just remember who walks with you; your Higher Power will help you through this tough time. I have been walking this path since 1982, and it has never let me down. It will not let you down, either. No matter what situation you are now facing, I say to you: Stay anchored, stay the course, this too shall pass. The clouds always give way to a blue sky. The sun will rise again and you will find a job. Life will return to normal.

At this point, let me offer you a suggestion. When things settle down for you and life returns to some semblance of "normal" and you realize you've gotten through your present hardship, start looking for something that you can do for yourself. Pursue a new hobby or learn a new skill that you could do if tough times knock again on your door. Jobs, even careers can come and go. Tap into something you love and can do well. It's good to know how to do something that people will always need. There will always be a need for people who can do things with their hands—barbers, carpenters, typists, landscapers, wallpapers. You figure it out, pick up a valuable skill, and never be caught in this position again. Let me continue by telling you a little story.

It's a story about something I saw that told me I needed to go after my lifelong dream. It happened more than five years ago, shortly after my dream was planted in my mind.

I took a business trip out to Lake Tahoe with a friend of mine named Dick Hanson in June 1999. As with most business trips, we had several meetings punctuated with long periods of waiting. The good thing about traveling with Dick is that he likes to spend as much time as he can seeing everything possible. And we did.

On one trip into the mountains, as we were driving along, something arrested my attention. Growing out of the mountain stood a pine tree at least fifty feet tall. It was a beautiful sight, but something didn't look right about it.

So I turned to him and said, "Dick, stop for a minute. I want to have a look at something we just passed." He humored me and backed up, so I could get out and have a look.

This tree grew right out of a cleft in the rock, alone. No trees stood near it, not within fifty feet or more. I couldn't see any dirt or water, nothing to support or sustain it. It simply stood alone—the same way we must, at times.

## Anchors

"How is this possible," I asked myself. "How did this tree survive against all the elements: the rain, the snow, the wind? How did it grow from a small seed, standing alone, withstand all the weather thrown against it, and grow to be fifty feet tall? What did it anchor itself to when the storms came?"

I looked more closely, examining the cleft it was growing from, at the bottom of which must be soil, water, and nutrients, but I couldn't see it. No support system for this tree could readily be found.

California redwood trees grow to be large and tall and live for a long time against the elements. One reason for their strength and long life is found in their roots. The roots systems of neighboring trees interlock and overgrow each other, which gives the whole stand added strength that holds them together when the wind starts blowing and the bad weather sets in. Yet this tree was standing alone.

I believe the bottom line is that this tree survived because it was someone's will that this tree survive, call it God, call it the Universe, call it what you will, but this tree survived against everything because it had a hidden anchor.

What an anchor does is hold something in place. Many people feel that it draws them down, holds them back. No, that is what the storms do, whether they take the form of naysaying people, financial troubles, or other difficulties in life—but that is not the function of an anchor.

When a storm comes, you drop the anchor, and just like a ship, it will hold you in that same place until the storms subside and you're ready to continue on your journey. It's not something heavy or difficult to bear—anchors usually weigh a tiny fraction of what ships do. But they have that centering function when you put them into play. Just like the anchor of a ship. Make sure you have something to anchor to when things get rough.

If this tree—standing alone against all odds, with no other trees to help protect it or help hold it in place, existing on what must certainly be limited resources of all types—still survived and grew to be fifty feet tall, then what could keep me from pursuing my dream?

Nothing. I became so obsessed with this one tree that I made two more visits back to see it while I was on that trip. I looked for a water supply and found none. I tried to see around the bark of the trunk into the cleft of the rock and could not.

*Yet the tree survived.*

You must have an unseen support system in your life. Find it and hold onto it. For me, it's God. That's all I'm going to say, and I'm not going to bug you about finding religion. I'm not here to preach to you, nor am I here to tell you how to live your life.

My simple question for you today is just this: What anchors you when storms come raging into your life? Who or what do you turn to; who do you call upon; what do you believe in that will move you forward to action? It can be anything: yourself, a loved one, religion, a community. Just remember that if you put all your dependence upon people, they may let you down, or turn out to be the naysayers I talked about earlier. Be careful; look for support and strength in persons who are winners, who are willing to help you when things get tough.

You can't always see where a person is rooted, but if you are rooted and anchored well, you can withstand all the pressures life can throw at you. When the winds blow and the storms come, if you are anchored strongly enough to whatever you believe in, you will withstand what comes.

*Find your anchor.*

# Reminders

I will always hold the picture of this tree in my mind. It is a picture that reminds me that life is what we make of it, nothing more or less than that. And that tree reminds me that I was not doing all that I can do, not giving all that I have to give.

And that for us to truly live, we must, above everything in life, pursue our purpose in life.

That bears repeating, I think.

To truly live, we must, above everything in life, pursue our purpose in life. We must pursue our dreams. Otherwise, life is colorless and devoid of passion; we are shirking our mission and the purpose we showed up to do. Each one of us has something we are good at, which nearly almost always happens to be something we love to do, something that God, the Universe, or whatever you want to call the thing that gives order to the cosmos, has given us to do.

If you're not doing that one thing, you are wasting your life. Pull it back up on the table and deal with it, or it will stay in your face. You will grow old wishing you had pursued your dream. One of the greatest tragedies is to come to the end of your life and say, "I wish I had done that."

That tree reminded me I was not pursuing my life's dream. That day, I realized that I had to move myself to action. That day was the day of my significant emotional event. That was the day the book you hold in your hands and the life that wrote it began, because I realized I had an unaccomplished dream, and it was beginning to consume me. I knew this time the desire was not going to just go away. Something deep inside of me was stirring my nest, and I could not get it out of my mind.

Has something happened to you in your life to get your attention and spur you into action? It can be something as simple and symbolic as a tree, the American flag, or words in a book.

This tree reminded me that when you develop a passion for your dream, you will most often have to stand alone. But if you pursue and persist—and motivate yourself to action—you can realize your dream, and others will come to help you.

# A Deeper Belief

There's more, though. As I stood there watching this tree so majestic and alone, it moved me to an even deeper belief. I came to truly believe that you come to a point in life where your dreams begin to pursue you.

There comes a time when you can think of nothing else—when you wake up at night knowing you could do this thing as well as anyone out there, maybe better There comes a time when you may be moved to tears watching someone else do that thing *you* should be doing.

This is the point where you know there is no turning around, no playing with the idea, no tiptoeing through the tulips. God (or whatever—call it what you will) has given you the nod and is calling you into action, and you have to do it, or you will not get any peace.

A warning: Do not, and I say again, *do not* get this mixed up with thinking this will be easy. A significant emotional event does not mean you just wait and it comes. Deciding to do it is just getting out the door. The hardest door to get through is your own—but just because you've gotten through it doesn't mean the rest is downhill—it isn't.

This is just the beginning. Phase one. The real test is still to come. The question is: Can God or your Higher Power trust you to carry this dream to success? He's done his work. It's all on you now.

# Calling to You

But if you carry it through and cling to your anchor, you will find something true, and something interesting. Farther down the road, after you've worked at it, worked at it, and worked at it some more, you will start to get people knocking on your door asking you to give them speeches, e-mailing you to do some writing for them, leaving you phone messages asking you to sing at some event—whatever it is your dream is.

It begins to pursue you because it is a part of you. And once you've made it that far, you begin to see the possibility. You start thinking and believing, "I can do this." You begin to catch the vision, the spirit. This is especially when you must guard yourself against the negative comments of friends that say they just want to "help you."

Trust your gut. One thing that has been the most help to me throughout my life has been my intuition. When I reflect upon the various decisions I've made in my life, I see that whenever I let my Higher Power guide me, it always seems to have worked out. However, when I started trying to manage my assignments, my relationships, my career, it seems as though God took his hands off. In these cases, I always seemed to meet with difficult times.

I firmly believe that our creator has placed an instinct in us. For me it is my gut. When I get into certain situations, it sets off an alarm, raising a red flag. When I think about quitting before I have something better, the flag goes up. Don't quit. *Just don't quit.*

---

As you go along, remember the tree that grew to be fifty feet tall standing alone, and remember its lessons.

1. As Robert Schuller says, "Tough times never last, but tough people do."
2. At times, you will have to stand alone, and you must find an anchor to cling to.
3. You must keep in mind the event that spurred you to action.
4. You have to believe and trust that the dream will soon pursue you.

That tree became one of the driving forces of my life. If you can use it, or something like it, and make it yours, I think it will work for you, too.

# 7 | Seven Steps to Achieving Success

*The great thing in this world is not so much where we are, but in what direction we are moving.*

—Oliver Wendell Holmes

---

This chapter is about charting your course, finding your way through life. It's about knowing where you want to go and how you plan to get there. There is no train you can ride to easy success, and if there were, believe me, it would be overloaded with people wanting something for nothing. But the process itself can be divided into fairly easy to understand segments. This chapter presents seven steps to take in order to find your own, unique pathway.

## The Seven Steps to Being Somebody

**1. Purpose:** *Decide What You Want to Do*

At this point you have heard me ask you this quite a bit: What do you want to do? By now you have also probably listened to some of your best friends; you have had conversations with some of your most respected confidants. You might have read some motivational books and attended a few seminars. You might even have told some key people that you would like to be considered for a position that is coming open.

You are trying to determine what your next move should be, and you may be feeling anxious. You see people all around you moving ahead and you know that your present job—which might not even be so bad—is just not giving you what you want out of life.

However, when you are asked the question "What do you want?"

you are caught clueless. You are like a deer caught in a driver's headlights. In fact, you are somewhat embarrassed to be in the spotlight this way.

Am I right?

Yes.

But it's an important question: The first key to achieving your goals is defining and knowing what you really want and what makes you happy. Focus on your gifts, things you are good at or things you like to do. There are a thousand possibilities based on this one simple thing that you like to do.

Only a few people can define and articulate what they truly want. There are even fewer who are willing to do the hard work of building the roads and bridges to carry them to where they want to be.

Remember: You can do this! Your dream is possible, and you already possess everything you need to get started. The seed was planted in you long ago; all you have to do is nurture it. Your dream is closer now than you can possibly imagine. The place is *here*; the time is *now*. The first step is to identify your goal. Be specific; this is no time to fiddle around. Move now, today. Not tomorrow.

You need to be able to spot opportunities. Sometimes we miss opportunities because we're not sure what we're looking for. But once you have a vision in mind of what you want, you will recognize opportunities when they appear, and you'll be surprised at how many there are. They are all around us—just look for them!

Do you want to start a business? It's out there. Do you want to get a new job or move somewhere? *You can do it!*

What do you want?

Finding what you love simply comes to you, whether it comes by accident, trial and error, or experience. It makes no difference how you find out what you love to do, as long as it is something that gives you joy, pleasure, love, and happiness; something that will make you a good living; something that becomes your life's purpose; something that will bring you to the end of your life with pride behind you, happiness around you, and hope before you.

Get clear on this point, and you'll be on your way. It's the first question, and it's the most important: What do you want?

## 2. Passionate Commitment: *Pledge Yourself*

Making a commitment is a pledge to *do*. Generally speaking, "commitment" is an agreement binding yourself to some course of action. When I think of commitment, I think of taking responsibility. In fact, responsibility demands commitment. For example, when I entered the army as a private, I took an oath in which I promised to serve my country. I made a commitment for three years. It was expected that I would take the responsibility to serve and serve honorably, which I did. Commitment is a responsibility to see something through all the way, once you have chosen it.

I do not take commitment lightly. *Commitment* is the word I use for issues in my life that I take very seriously. There is no place for carefree indifference when I give my word to other people. You give it, you keep it. Among my commitments are my responsibilities to God, my family, my health, other personal and professional relationships, and treating everyone I meet with respect and dignity.

There is no option, no compromise. I follow through. I give it my very best. Why? Because it is no fun to be lied to. I have been burned financially and emotionally by people—even in my family and among my so-called friends. Before you make a commitment, think long and hard, do your homework, follow your intuition, and determine whether you can truly follow through, because you must take all commitments seriously. It is too late once you have made a decision, a promise that you are unable to follow through on.

There will come times in your life when something will be offered to you, and you will say "No thank you. I pass on this one." It might be the highest-paying job that you have ever been offered. But after you have made a commitment to your goal, and if you realize this would put your dreams on the sidelines, and if your instincts and your Higher Power are telling you, "No," then let it go. You won't be sorry.

It's your turn to be successful; be prepared for change. Your dream might indeed call for alterations in your life and daily routines. It will require total focus, the assistance of others, and possibly a change in location. Prove your commitment to your dream.

I made the commitment to write this book and launch my speaking career. Was it easy? Not at all. At the age of sixty-three, when everyone else is talking about retirement benefits and Social Security, I am launching my third career, chasing an opportunity I knew little or nothing about. I felt like an ant looking up at an elephant!

Lofty goals? Yes.

Tough? You bet.

Fear? Absolutely.

But is it possible? *Yes.*

What drove me to it? Simply put, my passion and obsession for speaking and my uncommon belief that I am able to help other people discover and live their dreams. After writing down what I wanted to do with the rest of my life, my passion became even stronger. I figured out the steps I needed to take and started mapping out my strategy. I got the ball rolling.

Making a commitment might indeed cause you to risk something—your money, your time, your reputation with others, *yourself.* Do something solid that shows you have invested in your dreams and goals. My commitment required my time, my money, and my hard work—I wrote volumes of speeches and pages for this book, spent hundreds of hours reading and writing down things that I wanted to say or hear, spent money on books, CDs, and tapes, then spent more money on business cards, brochures, and all the other things you need when you want to be in business.

You don't have lots of money to invest? Then invest your time. Go to the library, do research at bookstores, or meet with people who do what you want to do and get their advice. It does pay off. Remember what I keep telling you? If you work hard and stay focused, you will find the tools, the money, and even the contacts you need. You just have to make the commitment to recognize these opportunities as they appear and then follow up on them.

You need to keep moving, making progress. Be careful, because this is a tricky time in your life: Sometimes you don't have the guts to go on. On the other hand, you don't want to jump too fast—calculate your moves!—but remember, if you do not move soon, you could become complacent, or fear could move in and make you stay right where you are. Honor your commitment to your dream: Continue to do something every day toward your goal.

### 3. **Planning:** *Develop Goals, Plans, and a Timeline*

This step is often left out of motivational books. Why? A detailed plan is difficult and it is something most people do not do well. We are used to winging it or faking it until we make it. For instance, if I asked you to lay down this book—right this moment—and immediately write down what you want to do with the rest of your life, could you do it? Do you know where you want to go? Have you made a *plan* for how you can get there? Remember—first things first. Planning is a key step to achieving success. Don't skip it.

Your plan is your mental vision and the road map for your dream. This is the process that you will use to get to where you want to go. Your plan must be specific, achievable, and measurable. It must have a starting point, a set of directions, and checkpoints along the way. Your plan is your written guide to your dream—you should make six-month, one-year, and five-year written plans to help you remember where you're going and how to get there.

No one would put up a home without a blueprint. If you're going to build a deck or even something as simple as a tree house for your kids, the first thing you need is a plan, on paper, showing how it will be done, how much it will cost, how long the project will take, and how it will look when it's finished. If you want to take a trip, you don't just walk up to the airline ticket counter and say, "Give me a ticket." The agent will ask you, "Where would you like to go?" Life asks you the same question: *Where do you want to go?*

As I said at the beginning of this book, most people spend more time planning a Super Bowl party than they do planning for their dream—and then they don't understand why they aren't successful. Whether or not a dream becomes reality depends on the details. Like a recipe, you must start with quality ingredients and follow all the steps in order to have the finished product. Planning is the most important step if you hope to achieve your goals. It's very simple. To get where you want to be, you need a well-thought-out plan.

Have you ever set real life-changing goals? Do you know how? Would you like to have a little help?

A goal is the target at which you point your life. Set your priorities and goals, and everything else will fall into place. Take a dream, write it down, set a date for completion, and it becomes a goal.

Let me give you some examples from my life. I have always wanted to become a professional and well-known motivational speaker. The day I recognized that I truly wanted it was the day it became my goal.

I recognized that I had a gift for speaking. In the army and in other jobs, this gift has served me well; people listened to me, and I could help motivate them with my words. I also realized that I *like* doing this. I received a lot of feedback and praise when I did it. Motivating people had a positive effect on me, as well.

I started looking for opportunities to speak; even as I performed my other jobs and commitments, I stretched for new opportunities. I looked for them.

I started to hone my speaking skills. I began to really pay attention to people who are professional speakers doing what I wanted to do. I noticed their style, the way they move around as they speak, their tone of voice, the kinds of examples they gave. I attended seminars and lectures; sometimes I didn't pay much attention to the subject, because I was so busy watching the way people spoke. Then I began to tell myself, "Lin, you can do better than they can." After several of my own speaking engagements, people in the audience began to ask me why I wasn't doing this full-time and for a living. At that point, the dream began to chase *me*.

Remember to keep your goals simple. Don't complicate it; don't feel that you have to understand and do too many things at once. Take it one step at a time.

Look around you. It is the simple things that lead you to success. If you are looking for other opportunities, it is probably because you are unhappy with what you are doing.

Less than 10 percent of us really set goals, write them down, and develop a passion for what we want. And you know what? That 10 percent achieve more in the long run than the rest of us. Isn't it clear that setting goals could help you become successful?

Now, sit down and write a detailed plan for reaching your goal. It's best to put it on paper. If you're having trouble writing it, then try first to picture it in your mind, with enough detail so that you have a clear path to take you where you want to go. To make a solid plan, you must answer the following questions: Who, what, when, where, how, and why?

**Who?** Obviously you. You are the one who is in charge of your life; what you do with it is your decision alone.

**What?** What is your goal, your dream, your passion? What do you want to do? Visualize yourself doing what makes you happy, because that will help you decide on the rest of the plan.

**When?** When do you want it to happen? And when will you begin? Set a date and get moving. Do something every day to bring you closer to your goals.

**Where?** This is a tough one. Most of you will be able to stay where you are, but sometimes following your dreams means moving—changing locations, careers, lifestyles. Start at home and figure out where you have to be to do what you want.

**How?** What do you need to do to get the job done? Think in terms of simple steps. Personally, I don't trust myself to think in complexities; I prefer to think in simple terms. Why? Because I know that during my hourly and daily activities, I'm not going to be thinking about the entire, complex idea. The purpose of making a plan, or a road map, is to break a complex system into a series of simple steps that you can easily remember and accomplish.

So how do you find out how to make your plan? Research, research, research. If you know people who are in the field where you want to be, contact them and find out how they got started. Share your dream with others who believe in you, and soon you'll be building a team of people who are almost as committed as you are in helping you get where you want to be.

**Why?** Last, but not least, is this biggest question. If you can answer this question, you're well on your way. The "why" is what you answered the moment you picked up this book, or made the decision that you wanted to be somebody. There are many ways to answer this question. For me, it was because I wanted to *be somebody*, I wanted to help people, and this is what I believe I "showed up" to do—this is my purpose, my niche, my dream, my passion.

Remember, you must have a defined, focused image of what you want to happen, how you want to get there, what it will take to make it real. Without your own custom-made "blueprint" for success, you will have a hard time building your dream into reality. Get your plans set before you try to build, or you may find you left something out—

and what you left out might have been the most important piece of the puzzle, without which you cannot finish.

You need to set your goals, make your plan, and follow it. The planning is crucial. Once I knew what I wanted to do, I took a yellow legal pad and a red felt-tip pen and wrote out everything even remotely connected to my goal that entered my mind. Then I used the process of elimination until I had a list I felt good about. During this process, I thought of my mind as a workshop. After a final run-through, I had my five-year plan and paid close attention to the detailed strategies I laid out.

At this point, I would like to say something right up front to each of you reading this book: This is not make-believe. It will be hard work.

*If you do not take anything else away from this book, take this. Write it down in your mind and your heart:*

—Life is tough and negotiating it is not easy.
—"Easy" has never been, nor will it ever be, an option.
—Life will give you back what you put in. No more, no less.

Remember, no matter how hard you try, you will not get out of this life alive.

Anything you hope to be or to become starts in your mind. We become what we think, by allowing our thoughts, positive or negative, to occupy and dominate our minds. Our thoughts act as magnets, drawing us toward our life's outcome.

## 4. Preparation: *Implement Your Plan*

In my training, I was always taught that after careful analysis of the task or situation at hand, you should pick and utilize the best course of action, the best avenue of approach. Choose the course of action that will give you the greatest advantage and opportunity for success. For success to be achieved, action must be taken. My passion pushed me into a course of action—once my goals were clearly mapped out, I was able to step onto the path I had prepared.

I have found that when an opportunity presents itself, the needed tools will come to hand. In my case, I suddenly found myself coming into contact with people who could help me make my dream a reality. Once I began a course of action, I discovered that by placing your passion and obsession behind your dreams, you will find the confidence and courage to move to action.

How do you move to action? You just do it. It's time to put your money where your mouth is, to put the pedal to the metal, to step out into the world and let everyone see you and what you want to accomplish. Do what you've been dreaming, planning, and talking about. If you want to be a writer, then write. If you want to be a singer, sing. If you want to be a painter, paint. Only by moving to action will you accomplish anything. You have to put your plan, your goal, your self on the line, right out there where everybody can see it.

At this point, pause for a minute and look up from the book while you think about the following: To move forward, a decision has to be made. Steps must be taken to get the job done. You cannot rely on anyone else to do this for you. Others might be able to help you, but you must take full responsibility for your actions, for staying the course, for keeping the faith and trusting that you will reach your goal.

All you have to do is to move to action, do something—then, anything is possible. Don't skip this step. Having made a plan, you must follow through.

I would like to share with you how I move to action. My first step is always to seek answers from God. The second step is to lay out my strategy and my course of action as a timetable. I put down tasks, times, contacts, and project completion dates.

Here is how I plot my course and follow through when I purchase real estate. Before I buy any property, I first set the top limit that I would like to spend for it. Then, I visit the bank and get preapproved for that loan amount. I start looking in the newspapers and driving through the neighborhoods that I would like to purchase property in. I call the bank, my friends, my neighbors, plus doctors, lawyers, and other professionals. I give them my card and tell them what I am looking for. It is amazing what happens when you get preapproved and set a date. Having created a network of ten or twenty people, you have all those sets of eyes and ears to help you find opportunities. It has never failed me. I start getting calls right away. Why? Because people like to talk—they will tell you everything you need to know and more if you are willing to listen. If you work out your plan and move to action on what you want, stay consistent, and follow through, things will start to happen. There is no substitute for moving to action.

You say you might fail? Welcome to the human condition. We all fail sometimes, but if you truly want to succeed, you'll try until you get it right. Don't let anyone or anything stop you from pursuing it. Your own actions are what will make your dream a reality. No one else can do it for you. Remember: what matters is not the number of times that you have been knocked down—it is the number of times that you get back up that count.

Move forward and keep moving, because the next thing you know, you'll be standing in the circle of success.

## 5. Test Your Plan

It's time for you to test your theories, step up to the challenge, and put yourself on the line. You know what you have to do; now, it's time to do it. This is your maiden voyage. Truly, how you handle this step can make or break you. It can give you the wind you need to take off and stay in the air, and even if you are not completely successful, it can give you enough of a taste of success to give you the ambition to keep going.

By now you have your dream firmly fixed in your mind, and you've written your plan on how to achieve it. Now, don't be afraid to ask for what you want. Take the dream to your Higher Power and wait for the answer—the inner knowledge that this is what you were put here to do. Consult with your Higher Power and with supportive friends for wisdom, strength, knowledge, and understanding. Think clearly about your limitations, possibilities, weaknesses, and strengths.

Do a little "market research." Take the first step by talking about your new endeavor, giving a sample of it, putting it "out there" in low-key ways that can reassure you that it will work. In testing my motivational speaking career, I started with a small speech—and can you believe it? The first time I tried, I failed. That sent me back to the drawing board for some fine-tuning. I analyzed what went wrong, and then I tried it again. This time, the response was so overwhelming, I knew this was what I was meant to do with my life. You'll know when it's right.

Listen and learn. I started to listen to people who were doing what I wanted to do. I went to every motivational presentation, seminar, and workshop possible. I watched presentations by people already successful in the field, like Charles Swindoll, Zig Ziglar, Robert Schuller, Les Brown, and Wayne Dyer. I bought books, tapes, CDs, and followed these individuals daily. Then I wrote my own speeches and started speaking to every little group I could—in church, schools, work, and so on. Did it go well? Not always. I bombed a few times. Now I know this is part of the test, and I knew I had to ask myself: "Lin, how badly do you want to speak?"

The major testing of your dream is where you pull out all the stops and expose yourself to risk. I told the world I wanted to be a high-impact motivational speaker; I put myself on the line. My opportunity came with the annual Youth in Government conference, a group of sixty bright young people from around my state. I prepared, I spoke, and it was a huge success. I knew at that point I would meet the challenges before me.

From that presentation, four very important things happened.

First, that speech was videotaped by a professional, and that recording became my first demo tape; second, the tape was presented on local television for thirty days, with excellent, positive feedback— lots of people who saw the tape told me that the thoughts I'd shared were meaningful and deeply moving to them; third, the success of that presentation and the feedback gave me the courage, confidence, and faith I needed—it rekindled the fire within me; fourth, I got a series of speaking engagements based on my success at this one speech. It led to my first paid presentation: five hundred dollars for a twenty-minute speech.

I knew I was on my way. It felt fantastic!

So let me leave you with a few points to remember about testing your plan. This is the point where you can make some mistakes as you hone your skills, where you study the experts, and where you gain the confidence to move forward with a full commitment to your goals. Once you have tested and proved yourself, you can, in the words of Henry David Thoreau, "Go confidently in the direction of your dream. Live the life you have imagined."

### 6. Patience: *Stay Focused and Be Flexible*

It is difficult to tell someone how to stay focused. You must make a conscious decision to avoid distractions; it helps to keep a concrete image in your mind of something you care about deeply.

We live in a noisy world. We have to learn to deal with distractions and setbacks that come along every step of the way. Everyone wants to succeed at something, and one of the prime reasons that few of us ever achieve true success is because we find it hard to filter out the noise and distractions and simply stay focused on our true goal.

So how do we do that?

*Stay focused by keeping your eyes and mind on things you want, and off the things you don't want.* Is it easy? No—especially not at first—but "easy" is not an option, remember? Luckily, learning to focus your attentions gets easier with practice.

Here is how it works for me. I know you've heard that a picture is worth a thousand words. The book you are holding in your hands is my picture; its goal is to help you create your own picture of the success you deserve. You become what you hold in your mind, what you think about the most. Who we are is centered on the picture we paint of ourselves.

Knowing what I want has been a great stabilizer for me. I am a visual person. If I can see it, chances are I can do it. I know that my purpose is to help others. My mental image is of all the ways my audience can improve their lives and the lives of others by finding and pursuing their dreams. I think about how I can touch the minds and hearts of people in an inspirational way. *My picture is of you.*

I stay focused because I have developed a passion and an overwhelming obsession to become one of the best motivational speakers in the country.

Maintain a burning desire to achieve the goals before you, and work hard. Develop your passion; become obsessed with doing something every day to bring you closer to achieving success. I have learned that when I stay focused, someone invariably shows up and says, "I know someone who can help you." Or something happens that makes my pathway a little bit easier. Help appears precisely on time.

Lance Armstrong, one of the world's best cyclists, when asked why he is so good at what he does, says, "I am on my bike eight hours a day." He's found his niche, that thing he's good at, and he's developed his passion and pursued it with the obsession needed to become the best, to become somebody.

Keep your goal in sight. Know what you want. Keep the faith. Stay true to your purpose, and be willing to pay the price.

## 7. Persistence: *Don't Quit*

To stay on track, I have worked to hone the one trait all truly successful people have: *persistence.* At times, it is the one rope that has kept me from floating downstream. Persistence kicks in on many occasions, at three o'clock in the morning or on the job, and it tells me to stay the course, despite difficulties, obstacles, discouragement—even when family, friends, and coworkers might tell me to quit.

I have never heard or read about any successful person who did not face some kind of obstacle, difficulty, setback, struggle, or discouragement in his or her quest for success. I believe the hard times in life are what give successful people the grit to hang in when their dreams look impossible. They know if they can hold on until tomorrow, things will change. If you believe and hold on, things do change, hopefully for the better, if you're pursuing your dreams.

Some of you will tell me, "You don't know my story, my circumstances, my history." You're right, I don't. But this is what I do know: There are lots of people who are facing the same uphill struggle, or worse, and they're going to make it—so you can, too. It's not over until you tell yourself it's over.

Believe it or not, I have quit several times in my life. The temptation to quit is strong, and you have to be stronger still. This book you are reading survived my temptation to quit. Motivational speaking has been a dream of mine for more than fifteen years. Simply put, fear stopped me, held me back, made me think about quitting. I feared my communication skills were not good enough. I feared I couldn't speak in front of people. I feared no one would listen to me. I still sometimes wonder.

In 1995, I decided to quit. I stopped thinking about my dream; I avoided writing and speaking. I had been given one of the greatest opportunities of my life, to speak to a statewide organization of more than three hundred teachers. At the time, the audience I was especially wanting to speak to was high school and college students. What an amazing chance to get into the field I wanted! I knew if I could make the right impression, my speaking opportunities would be unlimited. I would never forget this opportunity.

The introduction was perfect, the reception wonderful. I got up and spoke. I completely missed the target, blew it, froze. I gave the shortest and worst speech of my life, and I knew it from the moment I opened my mouth. I could have crawled under the stage. The worst thing was I had to remain at the head table until the completion of the event. The only thing I could think of was three hundred pairs of eyes staring at me.

That night I left the hotel, went home, and threw my manuscript, speeches, and my dreams into a box. I told myself this was not God's purpose for me, not my real dream or goal. You see, I learned that night that success is when opportunity, hard work, and preparation meet. In this case, the opportunity was there, but the hard work and preparation were not. Leave out either one, and you are doomed to failure. You see, fear can paralyze you. It can stop you in your tracks if you let it; it will make you give up and Quit with a capital Q.

I quit for two years, but then I found I couldn't keep from trying. I started giving small presentations whenever the occasion arose, and because I was now ready for success, I did well and the word got out that I was a good speaker. More people started asking me to address their groups, staff meetings, and diversity seminars. The flame ignited again. And here I am.

I give you a road map to success that has worked for me. Whatever you choose, if you follow the directions laid out in this book with a strong desire and passion for what you want and the belief that you can achieve it, you will arrive successfully at your destination.

If you do not plan your life, someone or some situation will. Make sure that the life you live is the result of plans you have made. Be careful how you live. Make the most of your time. Know what you want to do. Have a plan, know the plan, and work your plan.

Early in my childhood, I realized that I needed to find my place in the world, a place where I could make a difference in a way that felt right for me. I spent thirty years in the army. I cannot remember a day that I did not think that being in the army was right for me. I knew it; I felt it. I walked the walk and talked the talk. I stayed true to my dream.

I believe a Higher Power has put before each of us a purpose, a unique way of contributing to the beauty and goodness of this earth. I believe that God tells us that we do not have to go through life wondering and asking the questions, "Who am I?" "Why am I here?" "How do I get on the right road to understanding what is right for me?"

Getting this answer is *not* a simple process. It is tough. There are no simple answers that you can get by visiting the library, clicking on a web page, or taking a simple personality test. You cannot walk away with a checklist that will assure you a successful life or purpose. But God does possess the key that will help you find the combination to opening the door to your dream.

In the rest of this chapter, I will share with you a few steps I have followed over the years that have worked for me. As you use them, feel free to modify them or change them to fit your situation. Arriving successfully at your destination is what we have set out to do. Remember, there is only one *true north*. If you hope to arrive at your destination, you must have a plan tailored to your personal situation. You must believe in your plan and follow it. These steps have served as a road map for my life's accomplishments. For me, it always begins with my dissatisfaction with the status quo—my work, my relationships, my weight, my location, or just knowing in my gut that a change needs to take place.

# Getting Started

In 1983, it became pretty clear to me that I had become the major player in my daughter's life. The parent that would be responsible for the day-to-day, month-to-month, and year-to-year needs.

That thought had a very sobering effect on me. I faced a huge responsibility, and I was uncertain if I was prepared for it. I never thought I would have to go it alone.

It had become clear that a divorce would someday happen. My wife had moved out of the house and was living some fifteen hundred miles away. Our relationship was over. Although the hurt was gone, I still had to pull my life back together. I had to be a responsible and loving father, as well. But as for the marriage, Humpty Dumpty had fallen off the wall and all the wishing and hoping would not put him back together again. The fat lady had sung and the show was over.

I focused on my daughter. If I had to rate myself, today, on how I handled the situation with her, I would give myself a C. Barely a passing grade. With my wife, I would give us both a big, fat F. There isn't much for me to brag about during that time of my life.

If you are facing a similar situation, or some other difficulty, remember that sometimes things just happen. Sometimes things simply are not in your control. There is no one to blame. Sometimes you just lose control, and we lose something big. Yet over time, we may realize that's not all bad. It's okay! I know that my God hates divorces. I know that. However, I also have to think that he does not want people living together when things are just not right. He must know that sometimes things are over, mistakes are made, or perhaps it was just never meant to be.

I always thought that if there was a divorce, then certainly Linda would live with her mother. However, God saw it differently, and I will always be grateful that Linda stayed with me. He knew I needed Linda in my life. With this newfound responsibility—her—something changed in me. My whole outlook on life changed.

I was financially broke. In fact, I was so broke that if I'd walked by a bank, the alarm would have gone off. But much more devastating was the pain and fear I felt inside. I felt cold within; it was unlike anything I'd felt before. Even during my days as a combat soldier in Vietnam—I never felt quite this alone and afraid.

I was afraid of the things I would face in my future. I was thinking that I had failed as a husband. My marriage was over and I was left with nothing but my daughter.

Doubts crowded into my mind: Could I make it as a single parent? Could I rise to the occasion? I was in my midforties and I had suddenly lost a great deal of my self-confidence, my boldness, my desire to get out front and lead the pack.

# I Needed Help

I truly needed help and I did not know where to turn for it—or perhaps I was too proud to consider asking. I knew I needed help, but I was afraid to ask for it. Yet there was one person I could always trust: I went home to talk to my mother. One thing I truly respected about my mom was that she never told people what to do, but she was a great listener, one of the best I have ever known. At the end of our conversation, she reassured me that Linda would grow up to be a beautiful young woman and that the rest would work itself out. She said that I should keep my daughter and stay true to her.

How right she was.

After visiting my mother, I still did not know what I wanted to do, but I felt better just talking to her. I knew that I wanted to rebuild my life: I knew I loved my daughter; I knew I wanted to be a good father and a good role model for her. I wanted to make a difference in her life, my life, and the lives of everyone I would come in contact with. I knew I needed God, my Higher Power, and that I needed to become closer to Him. I wanted to continue to be an outstanding army officer and to make a difference in people's lives. I wanted to be financially independent. I had not been that broke since before I left home more than twenty years before. I did not like the feeling of having no money.

These goals were very important to me. I'd fallen behind in a lot of areas of my life, and I needed to catch up.

I set out to achieve them.

I started to read books. I had plenty of time to do this—I was broke and truly had no life. But I still had a strong desire to be some-body, and I had a daughter that looked up to me.

I read *Think and Grow Rich,* by Napoleon Hill; *Tough Times Never Last, but Tough People Do,* by Robert Schuller; and I read the Bible.

The Bible I read more than ever. I read the story of Joseph. I became fascinated and excited with his life; even when he was sold into slavery, someone wanted to put him in charge. I said, "If God did this for him, surely He could help me." And he did.

The really exciting thing was that everything I read, especially the Bible, told me that if I could believe, then things would start happening in my life. So I said, "I need help," and I was willing to try this. My thought was, "What is the worst thing that can happen?" So I just tried it.

# It Worked

It is *working*.

A set of goals and a plan to carry them out will work if you are willing to work them.

In five years, I had achieved everything I had written down and more: My goals with my daughter, my financial goals, my spiritual and personal goals.

Write down your goals. Write down your desires, your passions. Write down where you want to be five years from now. Keep the goal before you, put it on your refrigerator, or your bathroom mirror, or the dashboard of your car.

Now you know why, when I talk to people, I always seize any opportunity to ask the questions: "What do you want out of life?" "Are you getting what you want out of life?" "If not, why not?"

# Clarity

*The vision of your goal must be clear, concise, meaningful, and achievable.*

You must write your goal in the present tense, as though you have already achieved it.

The vision of your goal, the one you have chosen to follow, must be clear enough that you can write or verbalize it in a concise meaningful manner. Ask yourself these questions and answer them clearly:

—What do I want?
—What am I willing to give up?
—How do I plan to achieve it?
—Am I committed to getting it?

Write down each answer in a single sentence. We're not looking for perfection, just for earnest, sincere answers. We are building a house for success. This is the first blueprint. It can be changed. Remember, anything worth having or achieving requires not just planning, and not just hard work, but both.

# Process

*You must decide on a process by which to get where you want to go.*

You want to get started planning that process by looking at three to ten significant points in your life. Revisit things like your childhood, your grade school years, your first vacation, the book you most enjoyed, your favorite movie, a conversation with a mentor. Focus on the subjects that come up most often, the things you always talk about, the things all these significant events have in common.

For me, it all started with a trip to Fort Benning, Georgia. There I decided what I wanted to do and was able to develop a process of getting there.

Write your plan on one or two pages.

When your alarm goes off in the morning, you need to get up and move to action. When I joined the army and left Roberta, Georgia, for South Carolina, the only thing I could think of was that this had been my dream since the seventh grade. The only thing I wanted was my parents' approval and blessing that I was doing the right thing. When my father told me, "Go, and do well; keep God in your life; we will be praying for you; and your mother expects you to *be somebody,*" that was all I needed to hear. I stopped worrying and hoping I would make it, and I started thinking of the day I would complete basic training and return home with my uniform on. I also started to think of my next training, and where I would go from there.

I never, ever doubted that I would be on top of my act. It was something I wanted to do. I knew in my heart that I had God's and my parents' approval. My confidence grew stronger each day. I traveled to South Carolina with faith, and fear was not waiting for me at Fort Jackson when I arrived. The challenge was not easy, but God handled all the obstacles, and I finished among the top in my training company.

# Desire

*You need a will to make it happen.*

You must learn to believe, with total confidence, that you can achieve your goal, and you must act accordingly. Check your compass often to make sure that you are headed in the right direction. Your confidence must be overwhelming.

Don't be afraid to draw on or lean on the strength of your Higher Power, or the strength of others. Remember, you did not develop this dream alone.

While in a jail cell, the apostle Paul wrote something that applies to all of us, regardless of our religion. He wrote, "I can do all things through God." If you set your goal with the help of your Higher Power, then you only need to believe, move to action, keep from looking back, step off in faith . . . and leave the rest to God.

You must develop an overwhelming passion for reaching your goal. Be careful, because at some point you may enter the "no man's land" of equivocation. It is easy for people or circumstances to talk you out of trying.

Your passion for achieving your goal must be so strong that you are willing to risk it all. You must try with all that you are, with all of your desire, until your goal begins to pursue you.

Develop a sense of urgency. Start communicating with people who think like you, who are doing the same things you want to do. You must build a level of excitement around your goal such that other people will *want* to help you.

# Completion

*Make a checklist; make a timetable.*

Put your course of action on a timetable. Say to yourself, "I will complete this project within the next day (or week, or month—whatever is reasonable)." Then *write it down* so you can see it on a regular basis.

Setting a completion date is very important. When I started this book, things kept getting in my way because I did not have a completion date for the first draft. However, when I began to believe this book was possible, and others began to encourage me, I set a goal for myself to have a first draft written by fall of that year. I completed more in the six months leading up to that period than ever before. I did not hit that target date, but I was close—and I *did* it.

Set a date. Have someone else hold your feet to the fire. I was amazed at what happened when I set a date for the completion of the book. It was no longer an "idea," but a reality. I don't know why this realization came so slow for me. In the military, you live by a time-table. You must be on the parade field not later than a certain time. You must run the two miles under eighteen minutes, or you fail the test. Your goal must have a timetable for completion, or you are just marking time and going no place.

Mark your calendar, make your plans, and move to action!

# Humility

*Ask for and accept help.*

Don't be afraid to ask for help from your Higher Power and from others. You have to be bold and honest enough to say to yourself, "I can't do this alone." The best athletes in the world all have trainers, coaches, and others who help them. The best concert violinists have had countless lessons and continually practice to hone their skills. Even skilled carpenters have had hours and hours of training and studying. When an athlete steps out of the bleachers and onto the playing field, when a concertmaster strides out onto the concert stage, and when a carpenter rings the doorbell of someone who needs new cabinetry, each is taking a leap of faith. It is good to have leaned on others for the skills and confidence you'll need to follow through.

# Focus

*Stay true to your goals.*

Keep your eyes on the prize. Get up every morning and step before the mirror and tell yourself, "I have what it takes." Say: "My Higher Power has sanctioned this goal, and I will not allow anyone to turn me around."

When I finished my officer's training at Fort Benning, Georgia, and was commissioned as a second lieutenant, I immediately went out and bought a set of *captain's* bars. I put the bars inside my cap, so that anytime I removed it, the bars were visible to me. Thus, as soon as I'd become a second lieutenant, the goal of becoming a captain and commanding a company was always before me.

Establish a way to maintain consistency in the pursuit of your goals. If you have consistency, persistence, and commitment, you will achieve your goal more quickly than you otherwise might have. When I was promoted to the rank of captain, I immediately placed a major's gold leaf in my cap! Sure enough, I was picked and promoted two years earlier than my classmates.

Keep your eyes on the prize. Work your plan. You have the stamp of approval of your Higher Power. Stay true to your goals.

# Trials

*Be prepared for the struggles that will certainly come your way.*

Negative emotions, setbacks, criticism, roadblocks, fear, and anger at times will crash in like a storm. They will blow you around, frustrate you, tell you to give up. They will question your resolve, and at times, you will be brought to the edge of quitting.

Don't. Don't even go there.

You will face many situations in your drive for success that will challenge your body, heart, and soul. When I reach this point, I often draw on what one of my close friends, mentors, and top NCOs told me in combat. He said, "Lieutenant, no matter what happens, or how tough it gets out here, *never* let your men see you sweat. Keep control of your emotions. There will be plenty of opportunities for you to become emotional. You are the one they are depending on when they are scared, when things get really tough."

Stay focused.

# Take Action

For me, this book is a dream come true. As tough as it is for me to admit it, this book has been a vision of mine for the past fifteen years. I have held the dream for that many years. It is my hope that this book will inspire you to do what I did, only faster: *take action* to dig down deep in your soul and cause you to take a daring move in your life. The time has come to recognize that the old era has come to an end. The job that you once had or lost will never come again. The relationship is over. The store has closed. The past is over.

Accept it and take action to move ahead. No matter what your situation is, no matter how badly you may have been hurt, how long you have worked for the company, it is over. Remember, "this too will pass."

Every one of us, no matter what our age, has an idea or gift we should have already taken action on, but haven't. Maybe that gift or idea is to start your own business, join a youth group, lose weight and get fit, run for an elected office, or further your education. Maybe it is to quit smoking, stop drinking, or refrain from talking about other people. Maybe you have just become sick and tired of what you are doing for a living and need a change.

I don't know what's on your mind, but I do know that there is something—an idea, a dream, a goal—that you should have taken action on but have not. It is your best idea, and it just may be your Higher Power's idea. Take it from me—someone, maybe God, is stirring your nest.

Get off your idea right now! Stop sitting on it, and don't waste it. Begin *doing* something about it.

When I was in high school, college, and the Armed Forces Staff College, I must tell you that my written communication skills were less than perfect. I will never forget—there I was, employed by a university, and the position of vice president came open. I had proven time and time again that I ran the best department on campus. Motivating students is my gift. I was at that time—and I still am—one of the best at inspiring others to be all that they can be.

Several students, along with a good friend of mine, went to the president and recommended that I be considered for the position. The word came back indirectly, and the answer was, "No. He does not speak well. His communication skills are not good."

Now you can see why I have been considering this book for so long. Some very smart cookies have told me that I couldn't write and that I should not quit my day job.

What if I had believed them? . . . But I didn't! I asked for a little help, and here we are.

If you have a good idea, don't back off; don't run away, because it will not let you go.

So what do you do? You take action on the idea. Make a decision, move forward, ask for help, and never look back. Remember that today's decision will soon become tomorrow's reality. Make the commitment. Ask your Higher Power to roll the ball into your court and answer the question.

What will you do with it? Simple. Pick it up and understand that with every commitment comes the possibility of failure. Don't let the fear of failure, or the fear of what others might say about you, hold you back.

Take the risk. The greater tragedy would be to risk doing nothing and succeed: you would then be a success at nothing! Success from nothing is unearned and usually unappreciated. You have to desire something if you want to become somebody. Visualize your dream: "The me I see is the me I will be." It will not happen to you until you tell yourself it is possible: "I can do this." You have what it takes. Get off your assets and move to action!

In the end, you alone have the choice to quit or keep moving. Which one will you choose?

My favorite book says, "If you have faith as a mustard seed, you will say to the mountain, move! . . . And nothing will be impossible for you."

When I'm driving on the highway, I think about what I want my life to be like. I want to encourage, inspire, and motivate people to change their lives and get the best that this world has to offer. Why not?

I want to use life up. I want to be happy, and I want to help others to move into the circle of success.

Take action on your dream and watch how quickly success will come to you. If you have a good idea, don't waste it! Do something with it!

*Take action.*

# 8 | Baggage: Forgiveness Takes Care of a Lot

*"If your enemy is hungry, feed him; if he is thirsty, give him drink." . . . Do not be overcome by evil, but overcome evil with good.*

—Romans 12:20–21

When you're traveling, there are certain things you want to take with you, and there are other things you just don't want to carry. If you're on a long walk, do you want to carry two fifty-pound suitcases? When you're flying somewhere, isn't it easier to go through the airport and take a seat on the jet with a backpack and carry-on suitcase, rather than with three huge suitcases and a steamer trunk?

It's the same way in life. Residual feelings of guilt and anger from past situations can stay with you, and you can end up carrying them around like heavy suitcases. They weigh you down, tap your energy, and distract you from your goal. If you hold a grudge toward someone in your past—even someone who deserves your ire, you will not achieve your dream. Lack of forgiveness hurts the person that doesn't forgive more than the person that isn't forgiven.

*Think about it.*

The people you hold grudges for probably don't care much whether you blame them or not. Chances are they've probably moved on with their lives and are on the road to being happy. So who is it that's being weighed down with that big anchor of despair? *You.*

When you don't forgive, you're the one left carrying the baggage.

And it's you who has to try to carry that big, heavy suitcase of anger up that long ladder. You'll never make it unless you let go of it.

# You Did Me Wrong!

Some people like to carry around the fact that someone has done something wrong to them. Have you ever talked to someone like this? All they want to talk about is the thing that "messed up" their life, or the person they blame for what they're going through.

You know what? These people want it like this. They want to carry that baggage. They want to tell everyone about it. It gives them a sense that they're doing something about what's been done to them. It also gives them a convenient excuse for all sorts of things that go wrong in their lives: "I can't do anything because I'm a victim." Sometimes they hang onto the pain because they think keeping the memory alive will prevent them from ever being hurt in the future: "Never forget!" And they like the attention when others offer their sympathy. All their conversation, whether it's at the office, at a party, or at home in the living room, is, "Listen, can I tell you what happened to me?"

To make it worse, sometimes we have to *outdo* each other, topping the other guy's story with one of our own about how badly we've been hurt and how many times. But we have to get out of that mindset, because it's damaging not only to ourselves, but to all our friends as well.

Think of someone you know who is like this, who only wants to talk about how they've been hurt. Think about this person for a minute. This person just likes to bitch and moan about how someone did him or her wrong. For a while, you probably empathized with this person, but you realize that's all he or she wants to talk about. The complaining is getting old.

Have you got this person firmly in mind?

Now let me ask you a question: Do you like to be around this person?

When you talk about your grudges, this person is you.

# My Divorce

My divorce was an event that changed the course of my life. I am often reminded of the saying that my mother would use when things would go wrong: "Remember, Lin, life is not a bed of roses. Sometimes it is hard. It's more like a roller coaster—sometimes you're up, and sometimes you're down. You just have to ride it out." Little did I know that the ride would be so tough. It was a tremendously difficult experience; it challenged the very core of my soul.

Dealing with the pain of a divorce and single parenting changed my life. I now know why in the marriage ceremony we say "Until death do us part." Whoever wrote that must have experienced a divorce. When the marriage ended, on top of the other worries I've already mentioned was the worst part of all: not having a companion, a support base to help me through the tough times, someone to understand what my daughter was going through, someone to understand what I was going through.

At times I was a total basket case, panic stricken. Sometimes, while I was trying to hold on, I found myself begging and pleading with God that something would turn the experience around and we could all be together again.

On many different occasions, I promised myself and God that I would change, that I would become a model husband and father. I would change and bring home flowers and become a better mate. Perhaps that would make my wife come back.

On other days, I would be angry, telling anyone who would listen how bad life had treated me. At one point, someone pointed out to me that *anger* was just one letter short of *danger*. At times, I nearly crossed that boundary.

There were also days when the sun would set and I couldn't have told what I had done all day.

Then the day came when we had to talk about our daughter and the property—the little property we had left. I asked myself, "Where did all the minutes, hours, days, months, and years go?" At that moment, there was not much to show for the time spent.

I learned to live life solo.

Have you ever felt like this? The brook has dried up, but the pain goes on; it dawns on you that your life is a puzzle that you must put back together.

It would be nice if there were a manual that you could pull off the shelf, a book that could give you some kind of instruction on how to put the puzzle together. Luckily, I found one that was just right for me: the Bible. I read a lot of other books, too. I borrowed a saying from Dr. Robert Schuller: "Tough times never last, but tough people do." I have added a saying of my own, and that is, "If life is hard, then you have to live it hard."

I now have an idea of what John Newton felt when he wrote "Amazing Grace": Sometimes it truly is grace and grace alone that can keep you hanging on.

So I say to all of you who are experiencing tough times in your lives: No matter what the situation is, "This too will pass." Keep your head up. Ask your Higher Power for help, and believe that your cry will be heard. Hold on to what you've got (your children, your job, your friends), and don't quit. Remember the words of Job: "One day you will suffice."

Reverend Robert S. Schuller described this transformation: "The clouds will give way to a blue sky. The sun will shine bright again. You will hear birds singing. Spring will arrive and life will return to an unexpected level of joy, peace, love, and happiness. The relationship, the pain, the job, the tough time is over. Now where do you go from that point?

"You choose. You choose to live a great life."

## So What Do I Do about It in the Meantime?

The most honest thing I can say to you is *Get over it.* Did you expect me to say that? Is that a little harsh? I'm sorry, but when you talk about your troubles all the time, you bring everyone down. Remember hanging with the winners? Remember we want to be around people who do what we do and do it well? Have you noticed the winners don't talk about how badly they've been hurt?

That's because winners have a unique ability to get past their problems. They pick themselves up and go on, and they forget about their hurts. Why?

Because endlessly focusing on your hurts can't do anyone any good.

Oops. You're doing it again. I can hear you thinking, "Lin, you're wrong. What about that old phrase, 'Those who don't learn from history are doomed to repeat it'?"

I'm not telling you not to learn from your mistakes. You have to learn from your mistakes or you won't get to the next rung of your ladder. All I'm telling you is not to blame those people you're learning from. Do you hold grudges against your math textbook? Do you harbor hatred and anger toward some schoolteacher who taught you? You shouldn't, because you learned from these. And if you do, you need to follow the thoughts in this chapter.

My point is this: If you hold feelings of hatred, anger, or old blames, why are you dragging that around? Does it really make you happy?

# Forgive and Forget

Most major religions in the world have a statement about forgiving and forgetting. In the Bible, Christ said that he would "cast your sins into the sea . . . and remember them no more."

Forgive the error, and forget it. One of the greatest things you can do is forgive and forget.

Most people in this world can't do either one. They harbor grudges for years. But we must strive to let go. When we don't, *we are causing damage to ourselves.*

Some people have this odd phrase: "I'll forgive you, but I won't forget." How is this forgiveness? It isn't really. It's a way of being civil but hanging onto the grudge. But you can't have it both ways, friends. You have to either hold onto the grudge, or *make the commitment* to forgive. Yes, that's what I said. Make the commitment.

You see, making a commitment is a part of everything you do. To accomplish things, you make a commitment, and you carry it through.

Even after you make that commitment, it's not usually easy to forgive, but it can be done. It requires a conscious decision on the part of the forgiver, along the lines of: "I will forgive this guy I've been mad at for the last fifteen years," or "I make a conscious effort to let go of the nasty past between myself and that woman who stole my job seven years ago."

Make the effort. It's a part of taking the trash out of your life.

# Fear

It all boils down to that one thing, doesn't it? Fear. Each time we discuss a concept in this book, we end up coming back around to it. Fear is the primary thing that stops people from progressing and attaining what they want. But the second big thing that keeps people from progressing, keeps them from their dreams, and keeps them inside their own door is *that grudge* they can't let go of. But then, can't it be said that holding onto a grudge, too, is the result of fear?

I have a very good friend who never holds grudges. It's not in him to do so, and when something awful happens in his life, he does not spend time going on about how unfair the situation was; he simply turns toward the future and says, "What's next?" That's how he thinks.

That's what this book is all about, isn't it? Letting go of your fear, taking out the trash in your life, and finding out what's next.

I once worked for an organization whose top administrators consciously did me wrong. They fired me because I disagreed with certain members of the management. I lost my job over politics. Now I could go on telling people the name of this place and how you shouldn't have anything to do with it because the top cheeses are unfair to their employees and don't listen to their staff. I could fill this book with pages and pages of negative stuff, bragging—yes, I said *bragging*—about how bad they treated me. But I won't. Negative thinking is no longer a part of my life.

In fact, I always tell people it's the *best* thing that happened to me. I was able to stop worrying about what certain people thought of me. I was able to stop worrying about how to fix the troublesome situations that arose each workday. I was able to stop worrying, period, and seek something else that made me happier.

That's how I ended up in state government. Working for the state of Missouri was not a long-held dream, but it put me one step closer to my dream, and my experiences there have taught me a few things that I would need to achieve my dream.

Dropping the baggage was crucial in order for me to move forward quickly. Forgiving and forgetting will enable you to move forward faster, too.

# How Do I Do This?

How do you forgive someone who has truly done you wrong? This isn't easy: You have to take the first step. It's like two people holding guns at each other out of fear—there's that word again—that the other will shoot if I lower my gun first.

Well, in the words of many a great person, you just need to *get over it*. Yes, that's what I said. You have to get over it. Make a conscious decision to get over it and commit to it. Try this exercise.

Sit in a quiet place with no distractions and relax.

Next, raise both fists in front of you and clench them as tightly as you can. As you are doing this, place all of your hate and anger toward one specific person and one specific event into your doubled fists and hold onto those things as tightly as you can.

Now: open your fists and relax. As you do, feel all of your anger and resentment falling away.

Repeat this procedure as often as necessary. Let it go.

---

That's a first step. It can be the most difficult part, because so often we are unwilling to really let go. We don't want to open our hands and lose our anger, because we are afraid of what will happen. We *like* telling people about the bad stuff in our lives: It makes us feel proactive—like we're doing something about it. It makes us feel protected: "If I don't keep this firmly in mind, I'll get hurt again." While this may be true, in the long run that hurt will be nothing compared to the damage it will inflict on our futures if we insist on carrying it around all of our lives.

But we're not being proactive. Just the opposite! In fact, by being reactive, we're staying in one place because we're living in the past—we're stagnating.

So what is the next step? After you've followed through on your commitment and actively, honestly let go of your anger, comes the really difficult part: Forget about it.

Really, really let it go. After you've opened your hands and release your anger, don't stay there looking in the direction of hate and anger. Forget about them and go on to your next project. Turn your attention to something alive and growing. Turn your attention to your dream.

By not forgiving, we often do great harm to each other—and to ourselves. We can't put Humpty back together. We can only let go of the event and the feelings we harbor toward whoever pushed him off. Let it go.

I had a very difficult experience with this. I hate to sound like the kind of person I'm telling you not to be, but I hope that my example will help you see that I know what I'm talking about, because I've been there. My wife left me. She backed out of the driveway and left me and our daughter standing there watching her go, and for the longest time I was angry at her. She left me! She left me to raise our daughter all alone without any support or help, and I truly hated her for it for a long time.

But as time went by, I realized I couldn't live like that. So I tried several things. First, I tried to talk it out. I called her on the phone and tried to reach some kind of agreement, some kind of peace, but it didn't work—we didn't listen to one another. I tried to talk to my daughter about my feelings, but that was a bad idea and certainly didn't help. I tried to talk it out with my friends and family. I was even talking to myself. But none of this worked.

Perhaps if I had sought help from a neutral party—a counselor, therapist, or minister, for example—I could have come to terms with my situation more quickly. If you are experiencing serious emotional storms in your life, I encourage you to seek help from a qualified, compatible professional. Asking for help in such situations is a sign of wisdom, not weakness.

In my case, what finally helped was a letter. That's right. I sat down and wrote her a long letter. You see, in a letter, I got to say everything I needed to say, and no one could interrupt or offer me advice or tell me how wrong I was for saying things. Nothing could come between me and my feelings. And when the letter was finally finished, I felt like I'd dropped a hundred-pound rucksack. Putting it all onto paper,

I let go of everything—watched it fly away—and I was able to move on with my life. I was the one who needed to stop the bleeding, move on, and get over it.

This was a genuine turning point in my life.

Drop your baggage and move on.

*Take out the trash.*

# Why Forgive?

Don't I set myself up for another fall if I forgive? No. Here's an idea a friend of mine likes to use.

If you burn your hand, do you never go near fire and hate and fear fire for the rest of your life? Some people probably do that. But it's a very difficult way to live.

But if you can forgive the fire, you can use the fire to cook and keep you warm. And you pretty much forget that it burned you. This is not to say you should behave stupidly in the future. You remember what the fire is capable of and treat it accordingly. You don't stick your hand in it again.

But you forget the hurt.

It hurts too much not to forgive; you deprive yourself of all sorts of good, growing, positive things if you can't see anything but past pain, old anger, and regrets. Until you forgive, you can't get back on the road. On the issue of forgiveness, life has taught me to stop and listen to my heart before reacting to anyone that you feel has hurt or done you wrong. You have to become a doer not a talker. Anyone can talk, but only a few of us can just go out and do it. That is to forgive, forget, and get over it.

I cannot tell you that the person you love will return, or that someone who did you wrong will apologize. I cannot tell you that wrongs won't happen again in the future. However, I can promise you this: Your Higher Power will be with you every step of the way. Forgive, forget, and move on.

# Tyrone J. Flowers

If you had asked anyone who knew Tyrone J. Flowers when he was a child, "What do you think will happen to him?" that person would have responded: "He'll be dead or in jail by the time he's eighteen." But God and life had other plans for him.

Being born out of wedlock to teenage parents, Flowers, as a one-year-old baby, became a ward of the Jackson County Family Court and was placed in his grandmother's custody. Here he was raised with her own twelve children in a single-family home, having almost no contact with his father, who was murdered when Flowers was ten.

Flowers was raised in poverty. Because of the lack of space, Flowers not only shared a room with a number of family members, but also shared a twin-size bed with a family member. Often there wasn't enough food to go around, and Flowers would go to bed hungry. Sometimes a meal for Flowers was a sugar sandwich with a cup of sugar water. Flowers would often beg and steal food. He would show up at neighbors' houses during dinnertime, hoping that they would invite him in for a meal. Often they didn't.

Flowers wore clothing that didn't fit. When he wore holes in the bottoms of his shoes, he put a piece of cardboard in them, and when the shoes began to fall apart, he wrapped them in duct tape to hold them together.

For fun, Flowers played baseball using a stick or a pole as a bat, and because he didn't have a regular ball, he used rocks or balls of tape and caught them with his bare hands, since he didn't have a glove. For a football he would tape up a bundle of clothing.

From kindergarten through twelfth grade, Flowers spend 90 percent of his time separated from the other students. He was expelled from school in preschool and in third grade, and from the third grade through the eleventh grade, school for him consisted of special education classes with children diagnosed with disorders. Educators never challenged him academically, he was never expected to achieve, and because his teachers felt he would not be successful academically, the possibility of college was never discussed.

After his family was labeled as dysfunctional, Flowers was removed from his grandmother's custody and placed in a foster home. Throughout most of his youth—from age seven to age seventeen—he was involved with the Juvenile Justice System. Over that ten-year period he experienced mental, physical, and emotional abuse while being shuffled among foster homes, private residential treatment facilities, group homes, detention centers, male reformatory schools, and state youth facilities. Flowers also had several stints in local and state hospitals for evaluations. He was diagnosed with Behavioral Disorder, Learning Disorder, Emotional Disorder, Attention Deficit

Disorder, and Attention Deficit Hyperactive Disorder; in attempts to control him, he was treated with medications such as Thorazine, Haldol, and Artane. When he turned seventeen, the juvenile system gave up hope and in essence told Tyrone to "go home and play basketball."

After he returned home after his years of what amounted to incarceration, the challenges continued and no one knew of the obstacles that Flowers was going through. He ran out of money for food before the end of the month, and often there were no utilities. Flowers had to boil water in order to take a hot bath. Again, in order to eat, Flowers had to steal food. So many adults had told him he would be a failure! Determined to prove them wrong, he played basketball for his high school team and attended night school to make up the credits he needed to graduate from high school. After a successful basketball season resulting in a few college offers, and after having met all the requirements for joining the armed services, just two weeks before his 1988 graduation, Tyrone was shot three times by a teammate.

Life's challenges continued; the shooting had left him a quadriplegic. Revenge for his physical injuries was uppermost in his mind, but through the support of his church and the guidance of his pastor, his heart and soul were given to Christ in 1989. Flowers was able to forgive the young man who shot him, and today they have a healthy relationship.

The seed for his goal was planted, and he would not be deterred. He would serve high-risk urban youth, such as he had been, and help them overcome the challenges they faced. In 1991 he received his associate of arts degree from Penn Valley Community College, and in 1993 he graduated with honors from the University of Missouri–Columbia, earning a bachelor's in sociology with a minor in psychology. He continued with his education, receiving his juris doctorate in 1998 from the University of Missouri–Columbia School of Law, where he was awarded the CALI Excellence for the Future Award for the high quality of his work on children and the law.

After completing his summer practicum in 1993 at the Jackson County Family Court's largest secured residential facility, McCune School for Boys, he ascertained that a tremendous void existed in the availability of quality programs and services for high-risk urban youth. His goal took shape, and he founded SERVANT Programs in 1993; Tyrone incorporated the organization as Higher M-Pact in 1998. The mission of Higher M-Pact is to mentor, develop, and restore hope in the lives of high-risk urban youth—impacting the lives of between 40 and 125 youths on a daily basis.

In 1998, even though the salary was less than half of what Tyrone would have expected as a practicing attorney, to gain the experience he needed to achieve his goals, he accepted a position with the Jackson County Family Court (JCFC) as Deputy Juvenile Officer, one of the same agencies that had provided services for him as a youth. After working for JCFC for two years, he was promoted to the position of senior program manager.

In 2003 he accepted the challenge of a newly created position as a counselor, program, and service coordinator to the residents in the JCFC's detention facility. On a daily basis, he works with forty to sixty incarcerated, delinquent, abused, and neglected youth, providing programs and services they had not previously received.

His latest career move further prepares him for the challenges he faces as he serves youth through Higher M-Pact. By the end of 2003, Tyrone committed himself full-time to Higher M-Pact, and it was launched. As a result of years of planning, commitment, perseverance, and faith, Tyrone, his wife, Renee, and Higher M-Pact have reached a position to emerge as leaders in providing quality and effective programs and services to male high-risk urban youth in the Kansas City, Missouri, area and beyond.

Tyrone has certainly faced adversity. He could easily spend his time groaning about the hardships he has faced, placing the blame on society and countless individuals who failed or hurt him in his life. But he has let go of the baggage of the past and turned his attention to the present and

the future. Over the years, Tyrone has been featured in numerous publications and has received certificates and awards in recognition of the work he does for youth and for his community, and for his inspiring life story. Tyrone was recognized by the University of Missouri–Columbia School of Law for his accomplishments and received the School of Law's 2004 Distinguished Recent Graduate award. Tyrone's success has also been documented as part of Missouri's history in the book *"A Very Special Place in Life": The History of Juvenile Justice in Missouri.* He offers good advice to anyone wanting to *be somebody:*

> To reach your goals in life, you must first have faith in yourself and believe that you can do it. You must believe that you have all you need within you to get started, and trust that you will learn the things you need to know as you progress toward your goals in life. Always remember: "fear is perverted faith." Fear is having faith that the negative—the bad—is going to happen to you, instead of having faith that the positive will come into your life.
>
> Also, the road to success is not straight. There is a curve called Failure, a loop called Confusion, speed bumps called Friends, red lights called Enemies, caution lights called Family. You will have flats called Jobs. But, if you have a spare tire called Determination, an engine called Perseverance, insurance called Faith, and a driver called Jesus, you will make it to a place called Success.

# 9 | Fear, Procrastination, and Persistence

*Destiny is not a matter of chance; it is a matter of choice. It is not a thing to be waited for; it is a thing to be achieved.*

—William Jennings Bryan

Fear and Procrastination live across the street from Persistence. Don't get me wrong. Fear and Procrastination are not all bad. The three are very good friends—they hang out together, they go to the same church, shop at the same grocery store. They take vacations together; they cook out in the backyard together. They spend lots of time talking and discussing the world situation together. But Fear and Procrastination always find a way to needle Persistence. They call it "teasing," and they tell Persistence, "Don't take it personally—we like you."

They ask, "When are you going to slow down and enjoy your life—you have all the time [or money] you need."

"Why don't you retire? Join us and hang out at our little Wednesday talk group. We drink coffee and talk about everyone else in the neighborhood. We have a lot of fun. Come join us."

Persistence, on the other hand, is always moving forward, staying on the cutting edge of things, helping others. When you look around, you can see that Persistence has helped *all* of the successful people in the community: the pastor, the police chief, the principal, the teacher, the banker, the grocery store owner.

Persistence was around early in the morning and late at night, on weekends and holidays. Persistence was there with an offer to help the one that wanted to be successful.

To achieve success in your life, you must be prepared to receive it. Fear, if not controlled, will stop you from moving forward and cause you to turn back in midstream. Even though you were totally convinced two days or two weeks before that what you were thinking was the very thing you wanted to do, even though you *knew* it, Fear will shout at your back, "don't look down!"

And what do you do? You look down. Just for a moment.

And that moment's enough: You see yourself in midair and what happens? You focus on the space beneath you, and Fear paralyzes you. Now you can't move forward, and you can't go back.

# No Compromise

There can be no compromising between *fear* and *success.* You have to put fear in the proper perspective and be aware that we all suffer from it to different degrees. The only difference between a hero and a coward is that a hero gets out of his foxhole and tosses the grenade, and the coward remains in his hole and dies for his country. You will conquer fear only when you take action.

# Taking Action

No, it's not an easy thing, is it? Fear can creep in at *any time* during your journey toward your goal and whisper or shout, "don't look down!" and of course you look down, and then you find yourself frozen. You become lost in the No Man's Land we talked about in Chapter 4.

Now here's the big secret: Conquering fear does not mean you have to destroy your fear. Heroes are afraid too, just like cowards. What's the difference? The hero—you—takes action. The coward sits there, letting everything happen to him and *hopes*, against all odds, that things will somehow work out for him. He hides. But you take your future in your own hands, rather than letting it happen to you. Like the hero, you decide when, you decide where, you decide how.

Even if you're scared to death. You think that man jumping out of the foxhole isn't scared? Of course he is. People are shooting at him and throwing grenades and firing mortars at him. There's noise and bright lights and chaos all around him—yet he stands up and throws that grenade.

To conquer your fear you must do what you know you must do despite the fear. When you move yourself to action, only then does fear creep away.

How many times have you heard people say, "I've got to stop talking about it and do it"? We've all said it at one point or another in our lives, about big things or small, things we want to do or things we have to do. It's the phrase that indicates fear. What makes people talk about doing something but never finish it? They obviously want it, but they don't do it. You see it every day. The waiter who has the idea for a screenplay. The housewife who has always wanted to paint, but doesn't go out and buy the materials. The programmer who has always wanted to bike across America. The teen who has always wanted to go bungee jumping. None of them ever do it. Why? . . . Fear. They are paralyzed and cannot take action. *You* must take action *anyway.*

How do you do this?

We've talked about this before.

## Self-Motivation

A lot of this book may seem repetitive to you. That's okay, because there are certain concepts that bear repeating.

How do you overcome fear and inertia and take action? When fear grabs your attention, how do you become the hero and not the coward? There are two answers: Faith, which we have discussed at length, and habit.

Faith can motivate you when nothing else will. You must let faith take over your worldview. It is a conscious choice that you make. I wrote about faith in Chapter 4. I am not a psychologist, a psychiatrist, or a minister. I know little about faith beyond how it is working in my life. As Napoleon Hill tells us in *Think and Grow Rich*, faith is the starting point of receiving all the things that you want: "Faith is the basis of all 'miracles.' It is the element, the 'chemical,' that, when mixed with 'prayer,' gives direct communication with infinite intelligence." My belief has brought me to the realization that whatever I repeat to myself, whether it's real or not, will manifest itself in my life. What I think about the most, sooner or later, ends up becoming my reality. The thought itself acts as a magnet drawing my actions to what is in my mind.

Faith is something you believe in even though you cannot see it. Various religions ask us to walk by faith, not by light. I think that any "miraculous" experience in life is produced through this state of mind.

Martin Luther King Jr. worked in faith, which gave him the power—where others before him had failed—to move this country in an important new direction. Faith is the fuel needed for true success. Faith is the key that unlocks the power of your thoughts.

## Fear, Procrastination, and Perseverance

All three of these words have played a big part on the stage of my life. All three were seated at the planning table and played significant parts at every turning point. It has become very clear to me that if I hope to achieve my goals I would have to separate these three words and treat fear and procrastination as the enemy.

This does not mean you are to be afraid of an enemy. What it means is that you have to study the enemy's strengths and the effects he can have on you. It is a mind game. As a former army officer, it's easy for me to see this in terms of military strategy.

If you want victory, you must read the enemy's book, study his strategies, methods, principles, and traits. You have to know how he thinks, how he fights, and what resources he has available. Your strategies, tactics, and defenses must be built around perseverance, persistence, and staying power.

Dreams come true when you build the right fire under your desires and move to action on one, two, or three sound ideas. Again: Do what you love, and love what you do. A strong desire is the wind you need to set sail.

You must believe that you can get over, around, or under the obstacles that face you. When you build your defenses on a strong desire and back them up with persistence, victory is assured.

**Fear** I wrote about fear in Chapter 4. Faith is the opposite of fear, and fear acts like nerve gas. Be careful of who you hang around with in the early stages when your idea is taking shape and when you're fanning your spark into a flame. People will quickly pour water on your dreams—they will tell you to give up the idea.

Buy yourself a little shop in the mall and sell chocolates. You can never be a "singer." Get a job in manufacturing, like your parents did. The competition is too keen. What if Whitney Houston, Alicia Keys, Madonna, Tiger Woods, and John Lennon had listened to these kinds of voices?

There are no limitations to the mind except those we acknowledge. You overcome fear by building an overwhelming desire for what you want. Your best defense against all fear is to recognize it when you come face-to-face with it and take action.

Having the right state of mind is your defense against the naysayers—whether the voices pop up in your own head or come from someone else.

**Procrastination** Procrastination is the habit of putting off until later things that you should be doing right now. It is the failure to take responsibility and accountability for what you know you should be doing.

To counter procrastination, you must develop a strong desire to hold on tight to the vision of your dream, believing that your Higher Power has given you this dream, this idea, this goal. Follow your dream with determination.

Procrastination can become the enemy in your mind that will rob you of everything without ever seeming a threat. It comes into your life as the perfect holding pattern, telling you that you still have time. Tomorrow is another day. Why rush?

Don't misunderstand. Sometimes delaying can be good, a very healthy thing to do. But just remember: Timing is everything. You wake up one day, and you are ten years older. Once time has passed, you cannot recapture it. It is gone.

Procrastinators can put off things they have to do and the things they want to do. As much as I hate to admit it, I must share with you that I am guilty of putting things off myself. For example, the book you are reading was a good idea in my mind fifteen years before its publication.

Why is it that we need approval or validation before we move forward with our good ideas? Why do we seek out advice from people who know *nothing* about what we want or what our Higher Power's plan is for us?

If you need validation, take your good ideas to your Higher Power. It will not lie to you. It will give you an honest answer—one you can take to the bank.

We have a tendency to explain our putting things off as laziness and a lack of self-discipline. The student puts off studying until the last minute and then tries to cram everything in during the last twenty-four hours. Only a few of us can do this. We bomb the test and make excuses. "I only wanted a C from this course." Not so. You really wanted an A.

You need to plan and work according to your plan. You must manage your projects, your goals, and your ideals as though you are building a house; make your plan carefully, accomplish each task in the correct order, and stick to the schedule.

The alternative to progress isn't pretty; as Charles Swindoll put it, "Your life is like an egg. You cannot remain an egg forever. You either have to hatch or you will rot."

To put an end to your procrastination, begin by answering these questions:

*First, reestablish your goals and desire to attain them:*
   —What do you want to do?
   —What will the end results look like?
   —What steps will it take to get what you want?
   —What are you doing about your dream, your purpose, your calling?
   —What is holding you back?
   —Have you made the decision and commitment to do what you want, or are you like an egg in a nest?

*Second, why is this important to you?*
   —What motivates you to do this?

—What will you achieve by completing this goal?
—Are you mentally prepared to receive this goal?

*Third, what is standing in your way?*
  —Do you have the power to change?
  —What do you need to complete the project?
  —What will it cost you if the project is not completed?

*Fourth, revisit your plan:*
  —Have you developed your plan and written it down?
  —Have you clarified your goals and main ideas?
  —Have you set a time schedule for completion of your goal?
  —Have you committed to managing your time?
  —Do you review your goals and ideas often, maybe daily, or weekly, or monthly?
  —Have you teamed up with someone who can help you, who is doing what you want to do?

*Fifth, have you gotten started?*
  —Have you moved out of your comfort zone?
  —Have you made a commitment and demonstrated it with some action?
  —Have you put procrastination away—sent it on a long vacation and changed your home address and telephone number? If not, why not?

**Perseverance** I have found that the best way to develop perseverance is to select a team of people who will hold your feet to the fire and encourage you to keep on keeping on. Perseverance, persistence, and success have a tendency to hang out at the same places, belong to the same church and clubs. They travel the same road, going in the same direction. I often see them working hand in hand, living at the same address.

Most people whom I have met, with the exception of a very few, wanted to succeed at something. I often wonder why, when you ask six-year-old children on their first day in school, they know exactly what it is they want to be. They can tell you with no hesitation and with perfect self-confidence: a fireman, a doctor, a nurse, a dancer.

Why is it that after years of education, high school and even college, students don't know what to say when you ask them, "What do you want?"

I would be surprised if two out of ten could articulate to you with the same confidence and conviction they did at the age of six. It's true that as one learns more about the world, the different career options multiply and one is faced with an overwhelming variety of possibilities. But why aren't young people revising their goals, instead of setting them aside altogether?

What happens? Where do we go wrong? What did we teach our kids for those twelve to sixteen years to soften their confidence and their desire to be somebody? Or do they just get bogged down in the day-to-day responsibilities of school, work, and so on?

---

In this book, I talk about success, knowing what you want, finding your calling, following your dream, doing what you love and loving what you do, getting started, never quitting, being persistent. All of this is a pattern that has run through my entire life. I have experienced it *all*. Sometimes negative and sometimes positive. However, this I have learned: There are very few instances of overnight success—for most of us, that will just not happen. I have learned over the years that if it is your calling, your Higher Power/God will cause you to choose "the road less traveled," and with perseverance it will bring out your true talents, your true destination.

I have observed a lot of successful people in my lifetime. Of those who made it to the top, some enjoyed their success, while others made it to the top of the ladder only to learn that it leaned against a barbed wire fence. Those who truly made it started out right. They developed a sense of purpose and understood that their dreams were their true calling.

On the other side of the coin, many reached a certain level of success, and then they hit a snag or a setback. Then what happens? (Remember Lin Appling and his divorce?) If you are not careful, discouragement slips in under the door. If the setbacks and discouragement go unchecked, then we settle for a level of success far below our capabilities. But you do not have to remain at that level, and if you do, it is your decision and no one else's.

The lack of patience, perseverance, or persistence stands at the top of the major reasons for failure. Inside of yourself, you will find the real reasons why most people do not achieve success.

The starting point for success is called desire, and perseverance is the thread that runs through the lives of successful people. Knowing what you want will help you in the development of persistence.

# Procrastination

How often have you heard people say, "I can't do anything about it," when faced with a difficult path, and they choose to procrastinate, to turn away? They can't help it. Being the coward who stays in the foxhole is natural to them. It's their first response, learned as a child from people who would help them out of certain situations if they put off action long enough.

It's a demon shared by many people, and it will keep you from achieving your dreams if you let it.

Don't let it. Take action on your dreams. Move forward on the things you want to achieve.

## Anything Is Possible (author unknown)

If there was ever a time to dare,
to make a difference,
to embark on something worth doing,
it is *now.*
Not for any grand cause, necessarily—
but for something that tugs at your
heart,
something that's your inspiration,
something that's your dream.

You owe it to yourself to make your
days here count.
*Have fun.*
*Dig deep.*
*Stretch.*
*Dream big.*

Know, though, that things worth doing
seldom come easy.
There will be good days.
And there will be bad days.
There will be times when you want to
turn around,
pack it up, and call it quits.
Those times tell you that you are
pushing yourself,
that you are not afraid to learn by
trying.

*Persist.*
Because with an idea,
determination,
and the right tools,
you can do great things.

Let your instincts,
your intellect,
and your heart guide you.

*Trust.*
Believe in the incredible power of the
human mind.
Of doing something that makes a
difference.
Of working hard.
Of laughing and hoping.
Of lazy afternoons
Of lasting friends.
Of all the things that will cross your
path this year.

The start of something new brings the
hope of something great.
*Anything is possible.*

# 10 | Your Attitude: It Will Make or Break You

*Whenever I have a problem or difficulty in business, or any other problem, I say, "That's good." And then I say, "Now, what's so good about it?" And then I find out how I can turn these disadvantages into advantages.*

—W. Clement Stone

Your attitude will make or break you. Remember, we do not live in a perfect world. Over the years, my life and my experiences repeatedly taught me this powerful lesson. Your attitude absolutely determines whether you'll be a success, and you need to learn and internalize the concept in order to progress toward your dream. Remember, we all make mistakes. *Your attitude will make or break you.*

Your day-to-day attitude toward life and toward others can bring your dreams within your reach. It can also keep you from ever achieving them. You see, I'm not the smartest guy in my little city, but I am among the most respected. Why? Because I am optimistic, and I'm kind to people. People notice that, and they like me for it.

Your attitude is your choice. Despite the fact that entire libraries have already been written on the subject, I firmly believe that this one aspect of your life—your attitude—cannot be talked about enough, and I would be remiss if I did not devote substantial time to the subject.

# Okay, When We Say "Attitude," What Are We Talking About?

We don't need a technical definition here, do we? Dozens of dictionaries have already done that for us. But I think in order to talk about it, we have to get a *feel* for what it is.

Your attitude shows up before you do. It reflects who and what you are and how you look at the world. Most importantly, your attitude often determines the attitudes of those around you.

The psychiatrist Karl Menninger said, "Your attitude is more important than facts." The way you look at life can take you a long way toward the success you desire, regardless of the realities of your current situation. If you have a good attitude, people remember you. If you have a good attitude, you can get yourself through adversity. It can increase your salary, your popularity, and your position. In short, your attitude can help you achieve your goals and dreams.

*Attitude is the way you look at life.* There are four types of attitude you have working for (or against) you. The first is your *general outlook.* I'm sure you have heard "Is the glass half full, or half empty?" dozens of times, but that is essentially what we are talking about. This is good old *optimism.* For the optimist, every day is a good day, everything that happens is something she can enjoy or learn from, and life—while not always a "bowl of cherries"—is generally a good experience, because the optimist remembers the view from the peak, which helps in enduring the darkest of valleys. The optimist has enough faith in herself to know—not to believe, but to *know*—that she will make it to the next peak, and that the sun is only a breath of wind away.

The next aspect of attitude is *enthusiasm.* Thoreau pointed out that too many of us lead lives of quiet desperation. Well, we also lead lives in which we go through the motions, hoping we will eventually come out on top. But hope is not enough. Not only must we have faith, but also we must meet life head-on; we must believe in ourselves so much that we are enthusiastic about what we do and have a bright attitude about ourselves and our days.

Third is *the way you treat people.* In your dealings with others, treat them as though they are important and special. All the people in your life, whether dear friends or people you see in the grocery store, are just like you—they have wants, desires, goals, and dreams, and if you treat them well and make them feel special, then they will, in most cases, do the same for you. And they will help you get what you want.

Many years ago, I decided that I would make it a point to *greet* people. I would touch their lives, even if it meant just a handshake and a smile. So I started going up to people I didn't know—in restaurants, stores, or waiting in a line—and I talked with them. I really talked with them, giving them a smile and an ear to listen. I am convinced that is a big part of the reason I am where I am, speaking and writing to you, helping you to take action to achieve your own dreams.

Sometimes you should treat other people as though they have your career in their hands. Some time ago, I spoke to a youth group and was introduced by a state senator who happened to be an old friend and a former employee. I half-jokingly told the students, "Be nice to the people who work for you. She used to work for me, and now that she's a senator, I work for her!"

The last aspect of attitude is *determination*. It is often this form of attitude that will get you to your dream. Don't confuse this with stubbornness. Stubbornness is similar to determination in that you keep getting up when you fall down, but stubbornness comes from anger. Determination comes from faith: the faith that you will succeed, the faith in yourself that you will overcome the odds, and the faith in God or your Higher Power that help will be brought to bear on your behalf.

Determination commands a strong focus on a single goal: Your dream. Faith will get you there.

---

All these forms of attitude are related to faith. It is faith in yourself or in your deity that keeps your courage up and running from day to day. Faith keeps you enthusiastic when things get difficult. Faith helps you treat other people well even if they treat you badly, and faith helps you get where you want to go and achieve your dream, even against the odds.

*Faith is the key to the whole thing.*

# Attitude in My Life

Let me give you a few illustrations of how my attitude has worked in my life.

In August 1985, I arrived at the headquarters of the second Reserve Officer Training Corps (ROTC) region, where I was to receive my last assignment in the U.S. Army. I was to be a professor of military science at a university. Now, the army had designated this particular program for closure because of the low number of commissioned officers and the poor performance of the cadets at advance camp and on active duty.

Before reporting to that assignment, I was told by my commanding general that being given that assignment was no reflection on me. I immediately replied, "General, I am a fixer. If you are going to close the program, why send *me* there?"

His only reply was, "Don't take it personally."

For many reasons, it was hard for me not to take it personally. First of all, this institution was one of our country's historically black colleges, a place where black students could earn a commission in the army and fulfill dreams so similar to the ones I had held at their age. And from all that I had read, it was an outstanding educational institution. Indeed, the university occupies a special place in my heart because it plays such an important role in black history, in my life, and in that of my daughter.

The early founders of the university, both black and white, many of whom were Civil War veterans, had made it possible for me to become a lieutenant colonel in the army. They were all "winners" under greater pressure than I would ever endure.

Yet when I asked one of my staff members why this school's ROTC program was not doing better, he jokingly said, "Sir, these guys do not believe in winning."

I decided right then and there that the program would not close on *my* watch. *Attitude.* A change of attitude had to take place.

In my opening remarks to my staff and the cadets, I announced, "I bring a *renewed attitude* to this university and this program. The founders of this university give me no options. This program will not—and I say again, *will not*—close on our watch. I fully expect that in the future, each of your attitudes will reflect that."

Turning the program around and changing the attitude of the staff and the cadets was not easy. Breaking from old behaviors and traditions is always a tough thing to do.

The way I won this war was through my demonstration of what I was trying to change. I kept driving home that I would never ask them to do anything that I was not willing to do myself.

You simply must believe that your attitude will determine your outcome on the way to your success. I told my cadets, "I will model in every respect that which I want from you." I approached that program with the same approach that I take with everything I do, with high and positive expectations. I told them that I believed in them, and that I expected their attitudes would reflect my belief and soon my belief would become their belief as well.

If you want to change behavior, you must instill a deep sense of belief, discipline, pride, self-confidence, and a will to win, and you must set a new record of achievement. You must model what you want your people and the organization to be like.

I was out in front of everything that I asked my staff and cadets to do, from formations at six in the morning to the five-mile runs. I taught, modeled, and demonstrated what I wanted the organization to be.

Did their performance improve? Yes, you bet.

We went on to write history. It was the result of three life-changing ingredients: *a positive expectation, a positive attitude, and a strong belief in what we were doing*. These three ingredients can and did make the difference between success and failure.

We demonstrated not only that our program could reform but also that we could set records among the top universities in the region and nation. I helped my cadets accomplish this by telling them what I expected, that I supported them, and that I believed in them. Then I stepped back and watched them rise to the occasion.

Stepping back was a mistake on my part, however. The program had come a long way. We were among the top programs in the region, establishing new records for the national program, but I became complacent and took my eyes off the prize. I had failed to remember the standards I had established upon my arrival. I had stopped holding myself to those standards and had put my trust in someone else. I retired and went to work for the institution, not my program.

Not long thereafter, I was called into the office of the university's president and was asked to step down because of what I thought was a misunderstanding.

It was an experience I will not forget. It was devastating. It paralyzed me. It was the first time in my life that I had been asked to resign from a job. That was a very humbling experience; it reminded me that your attitude and performance can make or break you.

In that instance, it broke me. For one hundred and twenty days.

Remembering a statement by Keith Harrell helped get me through that tough time: "Attitude is a treasure that lies within you . . . the good news is that you do not have to buy it. But you do have to develop it." And you have to earn it and keep it.

After I left that job, I could have chosen to blame others for my circumstances. I could have appealed to the president, saying, "I saved this program. I have served in the United States Army for thirty years, and I have an outstanding record. I have given six years to this university. This is unfair. I ask you not to do this to me."

I could have fought it, but instead, through all this heartache, I chose to be positive.

I chose to suck it up, move on with my life, and see what other things life could bring me. The next day, I started my campaign to get back on top.

Four months later—120 days to the mark—I was appointed to the governor's office as one of the deputy chiefs of staff for constituent services, a job that led me on to be appointed as the deputy for the Office of the Secretary of State—to that point, it was the highest-paying job of my career. Next, I was appointed as one of the five commissioners on the Missouri Public Service Commission.

I will always be grateful to two sets of people—the ones who asked me to step down, and the ones who gave me a second chance. Remember, when one door closes in life, two others will open. Stay positive, stay focused, and stay flexible. Wear life loosely. Lightning may strike at any time.

Attitude made all the difference for me, and it has for many others as well.

The same applies to you.

---

I've told you about my divorce; here, let me tell you how attitude helped me overcome that critical experience. I was married for nearly twenty years, and initially I thought we had a wonderful relationship. I would characterize the first eight years as good. We had our ups and downs, good and bad moments, days, and weeks, just like everyone else.

However, in the ninth year, things suddenly began to go wrong. Trust broke down, and we grew apart. I tried hard to maintain hope that something would happen to put everything back together—back the way it was. But things never got better; they grew progressively worse, until my wife moved out and left Linda and me.

I was simply stunned for a long time. I kept looking for reasons "why" and for people to blame, and I continued to feel sorry for myself. One day, though, I found myself participating in a five-mile run, and a thought came to my mind: *You have a daughter to raise. Get over it and get on with it, because your attitude will certainly affect her.*

So I started a five-year journey to get back on top, and the next five years became the most productive of my life. I realized these important facts of life: This is not a perfect world; your friendships are not "flawless"; those whom you love, work with, and cherish the most will make errors, fail you, or desert you—sometimes when you need them the most. Be strong, forgive them.

The world owes you nothing. Will we each face tough times? Of course. Part of our job is to get over it and move on. No one is perfect; we all make mistakes. So do not be afraid to admit it and ask for forgiveness.

No matter what your present situation is, your attitude will make or break you. It is your choice: What are you going to do?

## How I Improved My Attitude

I have almost always had a positive attitude about myself, my life, my family, my career. I have always wanted to *be somebody*. All my life, I have realized that I had a different attitude, a different approach, a different outlook on things. I always believed I would be somebody.

I learned early in life that one's attitude is important and it can make all the difference in life. This became clearer to me when I was in the toughest internal struggle in my life, after my divorce. I started listening to Robert Schuller's *Hour of Power*. He made a profound difference in my life. I picked up a phrase from him, a phrase he used when people asked him how he was. He would respond with, "I have never felt better." These three words, *never felt better*, became a part of me. I still use them.

Later I added one more word of my own: "peachy"—because my mother made the best peach ice cream in the world.

If you truly think about it, life is good, and if you put your mind to seeing the best in every situation, you can honestly say that life just does not get any better than this, because standing behind every difficult situation is an opportunity, a new possibility. Sometimes you have to look for it, but it's always there, and it's your choice. Obstacles become stepping stones in the path of the positive.

It is all in your attitude. Stop blaming others for your situation, for where you are in life. Dr. Robert Schuller led and inspired me to listen to other inspirational speakers. I read the following books; they helped me, and I wholeheartedly recommend them to you:

—*Tough Times Never Last but Tough People Do*, by Robert Schuller
—*Wisdom of the Ages*, by Wayne W. Dyer
—*Live above the Level of Mediocrity*, by Charles R. Swindoll
—*Think and Grow Rich*, by Napoleon Hill

These books, along with the teachings and living examples of men such as Mahatma Gandhi and Martin Luther King Jr., had a profound effect on me. They were doing what I wanted to do. They were the true experts in the field I have chosen. They gave me the motivation to keep on pressing forward. I would listen to these individuals all the time, focusing entirely on their words. I would not go anyplace without a tape, CD, or book. These speakers and their writings truly gave me my deepest desire to change and help other people to realize their dreams.

They encouraged me to hone my skills and contributed to my overwhelming desire to help others find out what they came to this earth to be and do. Zig Ziglar taught me, "You can get everything you want if you are willing to help enough people get what they want."

Remember, your attitude makes all the difference. It will open doors you could never imagine. Today, I truly feel that my mission in life is to help others develop a positive vision of themselves. If I can point to the one thing that made me what I am, it is my smile and positive attitude and outlook on life. I simply love life, and I live to pass this attitude along to others. It does not cost me anything besides a smile, but it truly, truly works. Your attitude is the cornerstone of your life and your success, and it is the perception and impression you leave on others.

It will make or break you.

I am very thankful that I was successful in passing this on to my daughter. She is wonderful. It is touching when you hear your child expressing a positive outlook in life and using some of your principles, traits, and words. I was swept away when I visited her at her job one time, and her coworkers told me, "She *is* this radio station—positive, upbeat, with a 'can-do' attitude."

There is no higher payback than to know you have had something to do with helping to shape a positive mental attitude in those whom you have been associated with and love, especially your children. Take it from me: *life doesn't get any better than that.*

---

Sometimes people ask me, "Lin, how can I improve my attitude toward other people? How can I be a person with the kind of good attitude that causes the people around me to develop the same?"

I tell them there is only one answer: "Practice—choose to be happy anyway." Is this hard? Yes.

However, it is what works.

Many people will tell you differently, but there is no magic key. You must practice it. You have to make a commitment. (Sound familiar?)

You see, it only takes a few dollars more to go first class.

Make a conscious decision and a personal commitment to improve your attitude, and be persistent. There are days when your attitude will drop. Deep. On those days, pick yourself up and keep going. Keep your attitude twice as high the next day.

If you are to achieve your dreams, you cannot afford to be down. There is no option here. Either you are in or you are out.

If you get nothing else from this book, remember this: *Your attitude will make or break you.*

I think it will *make* you. I am living proof.

You were born for this hour. Review your attitude about yourself. Believe in yourself; believe in your own attitude. Don't let your past set the stage for your future. You need to try.

You need to try even when people around you are telling you—as has been told to me many times in my life—"you don't have what it takes." Don't listen. Don't believe what you are hearing. I know that together, my God and I will make it.

And you can make it, too.

Just keep working on your skills. Keep on singing, speaking, or writing. Keep believing in yourself, and you will wake up one morning with a renewed way of thinking and knowing that you can do whatever you set your mind to.

*Keep your attitude positive.* Remember you were born to win, not to lose. Before you can win, you must believe that you are a winner. You must develop a winner's attitude. Get used to thinking of yourself as a winner. Speak and act like a winner. Dress like a winner. Walk like a winner. No matter what your situation, you need to get up every morning, as Les Brown says, "thinking and acting like what you want to be, and soon you will become what you act like." Let no one tell you any different. Stop comparing yourself to others. There, you will always see people with more than you have. That has always been so, and chances are good it always will be. Count your blessings and thank your Higher Power that you can achieve your goals. You can always go from where you are to where you want to be.

I never thought I could do something so hard. It takes a lot of guts to chart your own course and follow your dream. But if it is hard, then you have to learn to "do" it hard.

When you really and truly settle on your dream, things will start to happen. People will show up whom you have never met or known.

They will tell you things like, "I know someone who can help you."

Travel lightly, wear it loosely, stay flexible, and stay focused. Remember, your attitude will make or break you.

---

As a supplement to this chapter, I would encourage you to read Keith D. Harrell's book *Attitude Is Everything,* which is an excellent treatise on the subject.

## We Are in Charge of Our Attitudes
(author unknown)

The longer I live, the more I realize the impact of attitude on life. Attitude, to me, is more important than facts. It is more important than the past, than education, than money, than circumstances, than failures, than successes, than what other people think or say or do. It is more important than appearance, giftedness, or skill. It will make or break a company . . . a church . . . a home. The remarkable thing is that we have a choice every day regarding the attitude we will embrace for that day. We cannot change our past . . . we cannot change the fact that people will act in a certain way. We cannot change the inevitable. The only thing we can do is play on the one string we have, and that is our attitude. . . . I am convinced that life is 10 percent what happens to me and 90 percent how I react to it. And so it is with you. . . . *We are in charge of our attitudes.*

# 11 | The Temptation to Quit: Don't

*To really succeed in life, all you have to do is: (1) Get Started! And (2) Never Quit!*

—Robert H. Schuller

At the beginning of this book, I promised that I would not leave you. I promised to stay with you and to give you personal examples of how I achieved my goals, how I am now living my dream. I hope you have learned some things along the way.

The road toward your dream is not a straight, clear path. It is the long and winding road you've heard about. As we've already discussed, sometimes it takes you through or near a "No Man's Land" of doubt and procrastination. When you got through it the first time, that was only the first pass. It always comes back.

There are times in your path when you feel you're losing hope with what you're doing, losing faith in the system, losing your idealistic notion that other people are inherently good. These feelings are very common. Sometimes you get to a point where you don't see how you could possibly go forward, and you sit there, painted into a corner. Then that little devil comes and sits on your shoulder, and he asks, "Who told you that you could write a book? Who told you that you could get a Ph.D.? Who told you that you could be a dancer?"

Your mind is the playground of the enemy. Your mind is where everything starts. At the beginning of this book, we talked about getting started on pursuing your dream, and from Chapter 4 on, we have talked about how the enemy can get into your mind and drop those leaflets that say, "Give up."

During a war, both sides will drop propaganda, pamphlets that say things like, "We've got 250,000 infantry soldiers waiting for you, and you don't have a chance. You'll never make it. Give up." Why do armies print up brochures for one another? Because that's where winning and losing starts.

If you can win the war in your mind, then you've won. If you lose the battle in your mind, that's it. It's over.

It's *easier* to give up. It doesn't take any effort. The path of least resistance is to just stop, *quit*. Giving up is easy—it doesn't take any effort. You follow the road most traveled because you worry about what other people think of you. This way, success will certainly elude you. You'll wake up one morning and have more life behind you than in front of you. Then what? Then where? Who do you turn to?

It requires commitment and hard work to achieve your dreams.

On those difficult days when you're in a corner, on the days when you've lost faith and are sorely tempted to quit, it's hard not to take the easy way out. The world gets dark and you feel "there's no point in going on with this charade!" . . . But it's *not* a charade.

You can't fake commitment. You either pursue your dreams, or you do something else. Simply put, you do it, or you don't.

Quitting has become easier to do than ever before. Proof of this is all around us. One only has to notice the number of high school and college dropouts, divorces, bankruptcies, business closings, and so forth, to see it in action every day. Across the nation, high school dropout rates are heartbreaking. Quitting is too easy.

When I left home to enter the army, quitting was never an option in my mind. Throughout my life, when things got tough, I always turned to words that my father said. When I draw on these words, they always give me the power to hold on until the situation changes. Some of the words that come to mind (and I've discussed some of them before) are *faith, commitment, forgiveness, responsibility, vision, belief, focus,* and *determination.*

These words have the power to change things for the better or for the worse. Remember, words are not cheap—my father always seemed to have a way of choosing the right word to lift me up when I was depressed and looked like I might consider quitting something. Words can build bridges to your future. Words can move mountains.

There are times to talk, to listen, to sit still—and there are times to take action. Knowing and developing a passion for what you want will help you resist the temptation to quit. That is why it is so important for you to have a plan. It does not have to be a carefully written business plan (although that might help). Remember the story of Ed and Margie Imo—they had no formal business plan, but they knew what they wanted and had vision, belief, commitment, determination, and focus; their commitment to their goal made them pizza magnates with an empire that grew from one store to more than a hundred.

You don't start a trip from New York to California without a road map. You don't plan a trip to Europe, South America, or anywhere without deciding what cities you will visit, without purchasing a plane ticket or making travel arrangements. Why would you start something as important as a career or realizing a deeply held dream without a plan?

Remember, if you don't know where you're going, any road will take you there.

Do what you love, find a need and fill it, and never, ever consider quitting. I cannot overemphasize the importance of doing your homework before you make the first step. Just because someone else has been successful, that in itself is no assurance you will do the same.

The key to success is knowing what you want and having the guts to go after it. As I've discussed before, early on in my life, I knew I wanted to be in the army. When the opportunity presented itself, I showed up at training camp prepared physically, mentally, and spiritually, ready to learn, and with a can-do attitude.

There will be a number of times the devil comes to sit on your shoulder. To help protect yourself from quitting, develop a set of words that you can draw on. Let's talk about the words that have been a guiding light in my life. When things get really tough, I sit and repeat these words that give me strength.

---

The first word is **vision.**

I have heard it said that when people have no vision, no desire, they perish. When I entered the army, I was taught from day one that leadership begins with a clear vision. Having a clear vision of what you want is important. A vision is a picture of your future. If that picture of what you want is clear, it produces the passion and confidence that will keep the idea of quitting from entering your mind. Hold the vision to achieve success.

---

A second word that gives you the power to keep from quitting is **belief.**

Eleanor Roosevelt said, "The future belongs to those who believe in the beauty of their dreams." Belief is having faith in a thing you cannot see. When you believe in the vision of your goal, then you have built up an immunity against quitting. Whatever situation you face, no matter how dim the path looks, if you can keep believing, you are telling yourself that you and your Higher Power can handle the situation.

I am often reminded of a saying that was found carved in a brick wall of a basement by an unknown Jew hiding from Hitler's regime:

"I believe in the sun even when it is not shining.
I believe in love even when I do not feel it.
I believe in God even when He is silent."

That is the power of belief. Don't let anyone steal your dream.

---

The third word I would like to address is **focus.**

Stay focused on the things you want. Although this is easy to say, it is not necessarily easy to do, because there are many things competing for your time. But I say to you: Keep your eyes on the prize.

Charles Swindoll, in his book *Live above the Level of Mediocrity*, compared life to money: You work hard for it, and "you can spend it any way you wish, but you can spend it only once. Choosing one thing over all the rest throughout your life is difficult to do. This is especially true when the choices are so many and the possibilities are so close." He then points out that "life places before us hundreds of possibilities. Some are bad. Many are good. A few, the best. But each of us must decide, 'What is my choice? What is my reason for living?'

In other words, 'What priority takes first place in my life?'"

Decide what you want, and stay focused on it.

---

A fourth word has always helped me along my journey: **determination.**

I often try to understand why some people in this world succeed while others fail, why some people perform their jobs to the best of their abilities while others settle for "just getting by."

Many people sit around making excuses for not trying. They complain about themselves or how their family, their significant other or spouse, the system, their job, or the world in general has done them wrong. They say: "I never had a chance to succeed." "I was born in the wrong family." "I was born in the South." "I was born the wrong color" (or the wrong sex or age). "I had the wrong parents." "I didn't have enough money" (or schooling). "My wife" (or husband) "would not let me . . ."

What a tragedy! What a way to live a life.

This is especially sad when you consider that we live in the greatest country in the world, the one with the most opportunities for everyone—the one our people, our ancestors, have fought to make free. It's called "the American Dream" for a reason: This country is pregnant with opportunities! You just have to decide which one you want, and then have the determination to go for it.

If you catch yourself whining, wondering if you should quit, remind yourself: If other people can go from nothing to something, then *so can I.*

---

Quitting isn't an option for me, and it isn't an option for you, either. I truly believe that if there is something that you want to accomplish, and you have the passion and yet don't do it, then in your mind, you have quit before you even tried it. So what am I saying to you? Get back in the race; get back on the playing field; get back in the ring. It is not too late to put your goal back on the drawing board and make a commitment to see it through by staying focused on what you want.

To help you stay focused, let's review the following five questions. If you can't answer them, you are like a car with four flat tires. You are going nowhere; you are likely to become a quitter.

1. *Who are you?* Do you really know who you are?
2. *What is your present situation?* Have you done a personal assessment of your life situation? I mean your personal, professional, and family life—can you see it all clearly, objectively?
3. *How do you see your future?* When you look through the glasses of life, what do you see? Is the picture clear? Or is it blurred?
4. *What do you want?* This is the killer question, the one that will stop you in your tracks, make you cry, sweat, and tremble. What are your goals? What is your passion, your dream? What are you focused on? What is your passion for?
5. *What are you doing, then?* How are you working, each day, to accomplish your goals, your dream?

---

I am not arguing with you. I am just asking the questions that life itself will ask you, sooner or later. These are life-changing questions. They make the majority of people nervous. They make you sweat, and sometimes, if you are like me, they can make you cry. For most of us, these questions are hard because we do not have clear answers to them—they are hard questions. But if you can answer these questions truthfully, earnestly, clearly, confidently, then you have developed a strong immunity against quitting.

If you know who walks beside you, as you travel the path to your dreams, fear will be impossible and success will show up precisely on time. It works, if you let it. But you have got to know where it is that you want to go. Where do you want to be two years, three years, five years from now?

If you fail to hold yourself responsible or accountable for your own actions, a sense of victimhood and unaccountability slips in the back door and blurs your vision, your mind, your faith, your belief, and your determination. Before you know it, you are on the operating table with Doctor Quit and his team of nurses, who are removing what you thought were your passion, self-confidence, and pride, and replacing them with apathy.

Remember, life has no favorites. All of us can make it—and millions of us do. So can you! You will become what you think about the most, so decide what your goals are, prioritize them, and focus on them. Take one goal at a time. You can succeed, and you will! *Don't quit!*

Many years ago, when my father would overhear me whining or complaining about something, he would tell me, "Lin, one of these days you will *become* what you think and talk about the most." I didn't quite believe him then, but today, I find myself repeating his words. Just think about it: If your conversation dwells on the negative aspects of life, it stands to reason that you will soon become negative—the things you think and talk about the most.

My advice to you is to take these two words out of your vocabulary: *quit* and *quitter.* Put them away, and never use them in the context of achieving your goals.

---

I know how hard it can be sometimes. When everything seems to go wrong, the temptation to give up is strong. But I believe in the power of desire, hard work, and faith. These three lifted me from being broke to being financially independent, indeed, quite comfortable. Remember, I rebuilt my life three times. Desire, hard work, and faith can keep you from quitting when everything and everyone—sometimes the whole world—seems to be telling you to give up and turn back. When I come face-to-face with the enemies in my life—fear, procrastination, doubt, and the lack of confidence—I build my defenses around determination, a burning desire for what I want. I know I can and will work hard, and I back it all up with faith. Faith is your starting point, your true north. Faith can turn your life around when you think that you have failed.

Faith is what you need when people, situations, or habits start to creep in, unnoticed, unchecked, to choke out your desire to go forward. Sometimes they arrive camouflaged as your best friends and family. Once they are in, they could cause significant damage to your beliefs.

If you find yourself looking for a way to hold on, when things get tough, *stay the course, stick to your plan,* and *stay away from people who propose to hold you back,* people who reinforce your negative thoughts.

As I have mentioned previously, there are plenty of people who can't wait to give you advice. Can't you just hear them now? "If I were you, this is what I would do." (Be careful, because this person is *not* you.) "I would not put up with that. They can't treat you that way." (Listen, only *you* can decide how much you're willing to put up with.) "I know someone who was in your same situation." (Exactly the same? Probably not.) "If I were you, I would quit." (Luckily, this person really isn't you, because quitters never get anywhere!)

Of course, *good* advice has always been and will always be a priceless treasure. However, win or lose, quit or hang in there, it's *your* choice whether or not to follow the advice people give you.

Whoever may be giving this advice—whether you asked for it or not—may know a lot about singing, modeling, cooking, finances, riding a motorcycle, or whatever, but before you take action, think it through.

Before you quit, *check it out.* Make sure the end results are your choice, not someone else's.

In most cases, the person telling you to quit knows little or nothing about the true power of desire, hard work, and faith—it's easy to underestimate the full force of these three, especially when they have been ignited with deeply felt passion.

In your quest for happiness and success, spend some time in developing your defenses against quitting. Build a habit of persistence, of not quitting. You will need courage, persistence, and determination to keep striving for what you want, especially during the times when it seems that everyone around you is laughing at your goals, criticizing your path, and showing little or no faith in you or your dream.

Remember, it is your choice: *Quit or keep going.*

At times it becomes clear: there are some things and situations in this life that are *not good for you.* If there are people and circumstances that are holding you back, tying you up, or beating you down, you need to get these people and situations out of your life—at least for now. Remember, you can walk faster with a friend who wants to go with you than you can with one around your neck.

# Reward and Punishment

We have talked a little bit about how we can alter our actions through rewards or punishment. This concept is called behaviorism. Modern psychology points out that there are many additional incentives for our various behaviors as well, but much of our behavior—more of it than you can imagine—is based on the simple idea of reward and punishment. Simply put, we chase for the things we want based on a promise of some kind of reward. We go to lectures in order to *get* something—knowledge, perhaps, or an opportunity to meet fellow students, or maybe just some free food. These are *rewards*. We often avoid dentist appointments because we associate them with pain: *punishment*.

When I first began to speak in public, I had a difficult time. Yes, difficulty comes to everyone. I had already had two careers, one in the military and one in state government, and I had gotten to a point where I was comfortable and making good money. I wasn't sure I could be a motivational speaker. Fear had gotten to me, the fear of failure—*punishment*. I had become conditioned to accept comfort and to avoid punishment.

It was not until I had spoken to several groups and realized that I could indeed help people that I began to work hard on the road to success with this new endeavor. I tasted the *reward of* helping people achieve their dreams, and I have been moving forward ever since.

There are thousands of examples. Think about your own life. Nearly everything you pursue or avoid is based on pursuing some kind of reward or avoiding some form of punishment.

And this leaves us open to *conditioning*.

The classic experiment of this was when Ivan Pavlov, a Russian physiologist, rang a bell every time he fed his dogs. After a while, the dogs would automatically salivate whenever he rang the bell—even when he didn't give them food. He had conditioned them to associate the sound of the bell with the receipt of food.

In the same way, we get conditioned to stop whenever the punishment seems too difficult.

When I was stationed in Asia and visited Thailand, I was told how they train elephants to perform in shows, to help with heavy lifting work, and to do many, many other things. When the elephants are small, they chain one of the elephant's legs to some large and immobile object such as a tree or boulder. When they try to move away from this object, the chain becomes tight and they can't move any farther; they stop. Try as they might, they cannot break the chain or drag the tree with them. They learn that they can't move away from it, and they stop trying. They become conditioned.

Ten years later, when the elephant is grown up and weighs two tons, the trainers don't tie him to a heavy object. They simply drive a small stake into the ground—a stake a ten-year-old boy could pull out of the ground—and chain the elephant's leg to it. The elephant has long since learned that when the chain gets tight, he can't go any farther, so he doesn't try to pull on it. When the chain tightens, he moves back to the stake. The elephant has become conditioned to let a small, wimpy stake hold him back.

*How have you allowed yourself to be conditioned?*

---

I have a good friend who is an excellent artist. He has painted a lot, but because he was afraid of rejection he didn't submit his work any where. He drew pictures—excellent pieces—but only his friends saw them because he was so conditioned to fear rejection; he always gave excuses of why he was not good enough. To this day, he works in an office, sitting in front of a computer all day to make a living, even though he's a brilliant artist. I think this is a form of quitting, don't you?

*What can you do if this kind of conditioning kicks in?*

# Reexamine Your Commitment

People can change, and their dreams with them. If you think you've been conditioned to believe in false limitations, try reevaluating your dream. If I were to return you to Chapter 1 and ask you, again, "What do you want?" what would you say? Is what you wrote down back there still on your mind? Do you still wake up at night wishing you could do it? Do you still feel sick at your stomach because there are so many others in the field who are not doing it as well as you know you could? Is it still a thing you love to do and something you would love doing?

If I were to ask you if this is still your dream, and you answer me, "Yes, but . . . ," then you need to *recommit*. It doesn't matter what comes after the "but"—it doesn't matter at all. Whatever follows the "but" is just a load of excuses, and we don't need to verbalize them. So you might as well leave off the "but." What do you have left? *"Yes."*

Recommit to your dream. It's hard, and it will require a conscious decision on your part. But there are *rewards* attached. Don't fear the punishments—yes, there will be some—but the rewards to come are much greater.

## Get Some Perspective

Most times, you start to think about quitting because of some form of setback. Something negative happens, or things aren't moving as fast as you want them to, or some powerful person where you want to be says No.

Think about your setback. Give some serious, rational thought to what's happened to you: Is it really the end of the world?

I don't mean to ask you that the way your parents asked it. Think about it: What is the worst that can happen as a result? I believe that you can get through that, and not only can you get through it, you can get through it easier than you think. Here is something else to chew on: Things rarely work out to the worst-case scenario. So if you can handle the worst, and things generally work out substantially better than the worst, then you'll be okay.

Your setback truly isn't the end of the world. The human animal almost always worries more than is necessary. It's part of our conditioning. . . . *You'll be okay.*

## Get with People Already Doing What You Want to Do

Here is another way to fend off the temptation to quit. At first, pursuing your dream can be a lonely proposition. You have to be self-motivated. But as you go along, you'll meet others who do this same thing, and through them you can witness the ecstasies and heart-breaks that go along with pursuing the dream. So get out there and network: Go to conventions. Join e-mail lists. Frequent bulletin boards on the Web. Find other people who do what you want to do, and hang out with the winners.

Finding other people who do what you do not only serves as a support group for those of you who do that special thing, but it also serves as a motivational group. What better way to get motivated to, say, improve your bowling than by hanging around other serious bowlers?

Hanging out with people who do what you love to do will help you achieve your goals. My father would often remind me that the company you keep soon becomes a part of your life. Your close circle of friends must be closely looked at. Do an earnest evaluation: Are you hanging out with people who do what you want to do? Are you hanging out with the winners?

## Take Care of Things Yourself

Is there anything more you could be doing to help ward off the temptation to quit? Yes. Get in the habit of being self-motivated. Remember when I suggested you buy yourself an alarm clock?

It helps to keep working at your dream on a regular schedule. Make it into a habit. Habits are hard to break, right? If you want to lose fifteen pounds, exercise at the same time every day. If you want to find all your ancestors, work at your genealogy on a regular schedule, at the same time every week, using the same space. Try to use a space that's exclusively for working on your dream. If you want to write a novel, write at the same time every day. Make it a habit, and your habits can carry you through the times you are tempted to give up.

## Take Out the Trash

Here's another way to keep yourself from wanting to give up: Take out the trash. All the extra junk in your life that draws your attention from your dream needs to go away. Order the priorities in your life.

It's been said that if you want to sculpt an elephant, you start by getting a big piece of marble and then chipping away everything that isn't an elephant. It's the same thing with working on your goals. If you want to be a singer, eliminate everything from your life that singers don't do.

Could I be suggesting that you dump your family? *No.*

Some families are very supportive, but others are not. The larger issue is, how can your family help you? Evaluate your situation and choose your friends outside your family accordingly. You cannot control the wind, but you can always control and adjust your sails.

# Exceptions

There are a few occasions when quitting is the right and honorable thing to do. These situations do not come up often, but when they do, you should be prepared for them. Of course these will be setbacks for your dream, and you must face that.

1. When you are being asked to do something that violates the law or your moral beliefs.
2. When what you are doing becomes so stressful that it is causing actual harm to your health or to the health of your loved ones.
3. When you have been asked to resign.
4. When you are going to be fired for reasons out of your control or for someone or something you should have caught.
5. When the company or organization you work for wants you to pick up and move overseas or across the country and you know such a move would not be in the best interests of your family.
6. When your health or that of someone in your family should be put first.
7. When love of another person prevents it.

When such a situation comes up, you should be ready to quit— but you should not give up trying. Devise a back-up plan, rework your path to success in another area, or join another firm that can move you toward your dream by an alternate route. . . . *And keep going!*

# Some Final Words on Quitting

You may recognize much of this advice from Chapter 1. It's true—it's my father's advice to me. This advice doesn't just apply right when you're getting started in your dream—it applies all the time you're on the road, and it applies even as you're arriving at your goal. When you put all these things together, they add up to a certain lesson that's very difficult to learn for many, many people: *"Easy" is not an option.*

Pursuing your dreams is always hard, but it's also always worth it. As you progress toward your goal, you will reach a certain point where you *know* that you're on the right track. Once you know you can do something, the only thing that can stop you is the temptation to quit.

And it's often this temptation that stops us. The temptation to give up is one of the biggest dream killers around. But if you can make it through this No Man's Land—every time it shows up—you can make it to your goal. It's not easy; was not meant to be easy. But it *is* possible.

If making it were easy, then everyone would already be living your dream, and there would be no room for you. But the way the world works, there's plenty of room at the top of that success ladder. The bottom is where it's crowded. That's where you run into hundreds and thousands of posers and "wannabes" when you start your dream. But as you work hard and start making progress, you leave the wannabes behind and discover there's more and more room for you.

Let's recap. How can you immunize yourself from the temptation to quit? Remember, this is a mind game. First, make your plan and be committed to it. It will help to keep words like *faith, commitment, forgiveness, responsibility, vision, belief, focus,* and *determination* at the tip of your tongue. Don't even entertain the idea of quitting. Know who you are, where you're at, what you want, and how you're going to attain it—have a vision for your future. Don't let anyone convince you to quit; hang around with people who do what you want to do. If things get tough, habits of determination, hard work, and faith can get you through. Be aware of how rewards and punishments can condition you to reach high—or not to reach at all. Use this knowledge of your own behavior to pump up your desires. Develop the habits of a winner—and winners certainly never quit.

If you hope to be successful, then at some point in your life you must break away from the crowd and start on a path of your own. Doing this does not make you independent or alone. It just sets you up to run with a smaller group of like-minded individuals. Sorry, but you can't take the whole group into the top 5 percent. This is another reason why I believe that no matter what your present situation, it is easy to win. There will always be less competition at the top. You can see farther up there, and you can help more people than ever before. With definite goals and the passion to reach the upper echelon, a person can travel much farther in a few years than he might otherwise in a lifetime.

I have one more piece of advice to give to you about not quitting: *have courage.* Put away your thoughts of quitting. The time is now and the place is here: Go for it. Make the choice—and keep making the choice—to follow your dream.

*You* can *win, and you* will.

# 12 Building Your Dream: Putting It All Together

*Let us, then, be up and doing,*
*With a heart for any fate;*
*Still achieving, still pursuing,*
*Learn to labor and to wait.*

—Henry Wadsworth Longfellow

---

Congratulations, you have arrived at the final chapter. Hopefully, this book has energized you take the necessary steps to live your own success story. Set the date and the time to begin your journey. Your opportunity begins here and now. Step up to the front ranks, select what you want, create your plan, put your plan into action, and follow through with passion and persistence. Now is the time to establish your goals and pursue them. Tell the world what you intend to do and follow through.

You will have to make some hard decisions along the way. If you are not careful, you might fall by the wayside; when things get tough, the temptation to quit is strong. But don't quit. It can also be easy to create excuses to not follow your dream—but if you believe in yourself, you will move on.

Now is the time to decide what you are going to do and where you'll go. Hopefully you have narrowed it down to the one, two, or three things that you want to do in life. During my short life on earth, coupled with everything I've read, heard, and experienced, there are three characteristics that separate highly successful people from those who are destined to a life of struggle and defeat. To lead a life of success, cultivate these things: (1) A definite purpose, a clear goal, a strong definition of what you desire. Nothing propels you in life as much as the certainty of knowing where you want to go, of knowing your purpose. (2) Your attitude. Remember, it will make or break you, and you must be vigilant against the psychological blows that can come from within and without. (3) Your determination. Remember, the road to success isn't easy; be committed to doing the hard work required to achieving your goals.

Put these three together in a positive way and you become almost unstoppable. However, pay special attention to number one: In my observation, most of the individuals I see failing and struggling in life are having difficulty because they do not have a well-defined goal or purpose. Let's face it—it's far too easy to give up, abandon our dreams, passions, and goals. To keep yourself going, you must know your answers to these questions: What do you really want? And what are you going to do to get it? W. Clement Stone put it this way: "A dream without a plan is only a wish." You must *believe it* and then take steps to go out and achieve your goal.

Some of you are already thinking up excuses: I don't have the time, the money, the education; I don't speak well, write well; I'm the wrong color, religion, sex. I've tried this before and it did not work. . . . You know, sometimes, there is merit in these excuses, but when it really comes down to success and failure, to where the rubber meets the road, these are clearly just excuses for not getting off the sofa. At this point let me make a suggestion: If you can forget the past, it is *gone*. Don't concern yourself anymore with opportunities you may have missed. Instead, reach out and take each new day as it comes. Ask yourself, "How can I best use this day?" Do this while you can, because your days will run out soon enough.

It is a matter of choice. To me, success is when you see an opportunity and willingly harness commitment, determination, persistence, and hard work to function as a team in your life. Failure will exit through the back door, and success will show up at your front door at just the right time.

Travel lightly. Wear it loosely. Stay focused and flexible. Sometimes, things are not readily visible. That is why it is important for you to share your dreams with others. They can help keep you on track. Although sometimes you can't see the total picture, that is no reason for you to think that success is not possible.

# Blueprint for Action

This is the *action* chapter. This is the point where you take everything you've read and heard and believed and make a decision. Are you going to put this book down and say, "Wow, if I were to do all this stuff, I *could* achieve my goals and live my dreams," or are you going to be the *hero* and take *action* on your own behalf?

If you don't like the way you are living now, or if you don't like the direction your life is headed, take a second look at the self-image you are holding in your mind. Remember, the picture you paint of yourself will determine your outcome in life. Only you can make that picture blurred or clear. Only you can make the difference.

*What do you want from life?*
— A more secure job
— A small business of your own
— A position in local, state, or federal government
— To pay off your credit cards
— To seriously develop a talent you hold dear
— To retire in one, five, ten years
— To attend college or to go back to finish a degree
— To take a year off from work

You work hard for your time, you earn it, you deserve it, you have the right to spend it any way you wish. This is *your life*. So what are you going to do?

Not an easy task to choose among the many options that are open to you during your lifetime; it can be very confusing, stressful, and difficult. However, isn't that what life is all about? Choosing? Keep your goals clear; keep asking yourself, "What do I want? How am I going to get it?" William Jennings Bryan put it this way: "Destiny is not a matter of chance. It is a matter of choice. It is not a thing to be waited for; it is a thing to be achieved."

Don't wait for your ship to come in—swim out and meet it.

What are the first priorities in your life? Answer this question and you are well on your way to knowing what you want. And once you know what you want, you take action, or, as the Nike company so bluntly puts it, "Just do it." Go out and take action, get it going, and *do it*.

It's not easy, and it's not meant to be. If it were easy, everyone would be doing it. But don't count yourself out just because the road has bumps on it. It's true that old habits are hard to break, and the majority of us have convinced ourselves that we lack the right stuff, that someone else gets to decide when we get the job, the promotion, the breaks in life. We tell ourselves that we can't do this or that, that we shouldn't take risks, that we are doing okay where we are. We have a good job with decent pay; so what if we hate it? We have the mind set that if we try, we are sure to fail, and failure hurts, so it's safer to not even try.

To overcome the fear of failure takes courage, endurance, and guts. When I was working in the educational system, I attended a speech given by a man who would soon become the governor of Missouri, Mel Carnahan. It was an inspiring speech. I approached him afterwards and told him flat-out: "Mel, you need me," knowing that he was running for governor. I knew I could help him and in the process also do something I wanted to do—but at that point, I don't know what I would have said if he had asked me, "What can you do?" Instead of asking me that question, he merely smiled and replied, "Okay, come see me." Mel was a great man and made a tremendous impression on my life. I wanted to work with him, and I knew I had to have the courage to let him know that I could be somebody in his administration. I was afraid to fail, afraid he would say no, so it took courage and guts for me to step out there and tell the governor that he needed me. You know what? He gave me a break in life right when I needed it most. In a sense, I landed the job just from those three little words. I will always be grateful for that opportunity. It showed up on my doorstep precisely on time.

*What if I had not asked?*

Ever since I embarked on my journey of writing this book, my major concern has been "Can I write a book or make a speech that will make a *connection*—that will make a difference in someone's life? Not the total audience, but just one person." I know that if I answer "yes," then it's worth it. One person is all it takes to change the world.

# Three Points

If you cannot see success for yourself, how do you expect to achieve it? You've done your homework, completed your self-analysis. You've asked and answered all the questions. It is crystal clear to you that writing your book, singing your song, starting your business—whatever—will take you from where you are to where you want to be. This is your dream, your purpose, your passion. You've made the decision to go forward. You've made the connection. You know that God or your Higher Power and the universe are beckoning you on.

But a nagging question might still linger: "How do I know this is right for me?" To answer, keep in mind the following three points.

# Know and Believe

First, you do not have to see around the corner. You just need to step off with the faith that there is a plan for you. You will never, ever be forsaken. Believe it! Whatever your dream is, it's yours for the asking. If your goal is right and you believe in it, all you have to do is pursue it. A burning desire to be somebody is the starting point from which your dream is launched.

How do I know? When I speak to a group of people, I *know* I am fulfilling my purpose. I know without a doubt that motivating others is my purpose at this point in my life. It is my purpose to inspire others to take action on the opportunities this country has to offer. Your goals are only limited by your imagination, tenacity, desire, and initiative. It took me fifteen years to know that was my calling—Did I ever quit believing? No! Did I have to work hard and be flexible along the way? *Yes!*

# Commitment

You have made the commitment to move forward. There is no

turning around, but it's okay to look around you. Get some profound advice; talk to people who are doing what you want to do. It is okay to recheck your parachute. It is okay to change directions if it is not working for you. Just don't quit.

Once you make the commitment, there is no room for turning back, and there is even less room for failure. The plane is in the air. You will either learn to fly, or you will come down and never take the risk again. So why not go for it? Although you can't foresee everything on the road ahead of you, commitment can carry you past all the obstacles. You *can* sing the song, you *can* pass the test, you *can* get the job. Acquire a can-do attitude. There is no stopping you now.

I can hear you saying it again. I can hear you say, "Lin, I hear you, I have read your book, and I understand what you're saying. But it *cannot be that simple!* What's the catch? I ran for office and did not win. I tried for the job and failed. I went for the promotion and was turned down. I've tried this before, and it did not work for me." But I'm telling you: It *is* that simple. No more, no less.

Follow the formula: Get clear on what you want, do what you love, take out the trash, get rid of the negative thoughts, and put your faith in the center of your life. Then go out and seek what you want. Simply take forward steps, believing that you can succeed.

If a country boy like myself can do it, why can't you?

# Be Somebody

You've have been through all the training, you have consulted with the people you need to, and you know this is what you want to do. Right? You have prepared yourself for this. Now it's critical: *Take the steps.* You are out on center stage, the lights are on, your introduction has been given, and the curtains are rising. This is your moment! Don't turn back—don't quit.

If you are prepared and have worked hard for the opportunity, then don't worry. Everything you need will show up right at the time you need it. Believe that it will! It might take the form of meeting just the right person or getting a phone call or letter or some other form of news at just the right time. Someone will come up to you and say, "I know someone who has experience with your project. She can help you. She can record your CD for free." Your opportunity will come: be ready for it.

# The Seven Steps to Being Somebody

I wish I could tell each of you reading this book that once you have made the decision and mustered the strength to go forward that you are on the downhill slide and the rest will be easy.

But I can't say this, and I won't. Nothing worth having is easy. Some of you will turn back, no matter what I say, and that is fine—that will be your choice. But again, I want to remind you that you should go for your dream—because you *can* do it.

However, I know that some of my readers will take the "road less traveled" and follow through to become somebody. If you are like me, you will have no alternative. Our names have been called, and we must step forward. There can be no greater satisfaction than to do what you love and love what you do.

Let me summarize the seven steps that can help you *be somebody*.

**1. Purpose:** *Decide What You Want to Do*
Identify your goals and dreams. Know what you want out of life and be willing to ask for help in getting it. Find your niche, the thing you do well and love to do, and go for it. What is your passion?

**2. Passionate Commitment:** *Pledge Yourself*
Risk something. Commit time, money, and yourself to making your dreams come true. Preparation and hard work are all you'll need to make it work for you. Take full responsibility and accountability for making your dream come true.

**3. Planning:** *Develop Goals, Plans, and a Timeline*
You must have a vision of a starting point, a road map, and detailed checkpoints along the way to get to your final destination: success.

**4. Preparation:** *Implement Your Plan*
Today follow through with patience, confidence, and performance. You know where you're going and how you'll get there. You've in-

vested time, money, whatever it takes, and now, you just do it. Every day. Do something today, no matter how small, do something—make a phone call, visit the library, write a letter. Keep moving forward and step into the circle of success.

## 5. Test Your Plan

Start putting yourself out there in gradual ways to fine-tune your skills and gain exposure. Successes feed your passion; analysis of any less-successful ventures will help you improve. Start putting yourself on the line. You don't know your potential until you test it.

## 6. Patience: *Stay Focused and Be Flexible*

Keep your eye on the prize; anchor yourself in your dream and keep looking ahead. Maintain a burning desire to achieve your goals. Don't be afraid to ask for help.

## 7. Persistence: *Don't Quit*

Everyone faces obstacles, but when they arise, you just have to hold on until tomorrow. Fear can stop you in your tracks, but only if you let it. Being persistent doesn't mean you can't change. If what you are doing doesn't work, consider a change of plans, but *don't quit.* You can do better. Keep moving forward.

---

Know who you are, know what you want, and know who walks beside you when you face difficulties. When preparation, hard work, and passion encounter an opportunity, success shows up precisely on time.

Make your choices with knowledge, confidence, courage, determination, and commitment. Do it now, and don't quit. We are all given the chance to do something great with our lives—if we just go for it.

The keys to success that I have herein described are a rough blueprint to get you from that first big step to the finish line. Once you ring that starting bell, it can't be unrung. The time is now; the place is here: *It's your turn to be somebody.*

# About the Author

LIN APPLING was born in Roberta, Georgia, to a family of fourteen. He left home at nineteen to join the United States Army, where he rose (without a formal education) to the rank of Captain and went on to retire as a Lieutenant Colonel. He eventually earned his masters degree while working full-time as an army officer and raising his daughter, from the age of ten, as a single parent. Since his retirement from the army, he served as a Deputy Chief of Staff in the office of the late Governor Mel Carnahan and the Executive Deputy Secretary of State in the office of the Secretary of State. He is now a Commissioner at the Missouri Public Service Commission, a position he has held since May 2004.